Dedication:

This book is dedicated to my three adult children and my supportive husband.

Thank you all for being patient in this journey. You have followed the path of your choosing and I am privileged to be a witness and sometimes companion. We are all growing and learning, forgiving and loving. You are my inspiration. Thank you for sharing your lives in your own way.

Contents

Introduction: Pour The Wine (Or A Hot Cuppa) vii

PART 1 – Understanding the Challenge 1

   1. Beyond the Empty Nest 3
   2. Research Evidence That We Are Not Alone 9

PART 2 – Who Are They? 17

   3. Their Journey to Find Themselves 19
   4. What's Their Work? 25
   5. Next Chapter Love… Life 29
   6. Not All Nests Are Empty 39

PART 3 – Who Are WE? 47

   7. You're Seeing Who? 49
   8. French Tucks and Other Lessons 55
   9. Sibling Rivalry 63
  10. Can We Be Friends? 71
  11. Holidays and Other Get-togethers 77
  12. Maybe Baby 85

PART 4 – Who Am I? 91

  13. Dangerous Expectations 93
  14. Values, Foundation, Grounding 103
  15. The Things We Do… and Don't Do 113
  16. Boundaries 123

17.	Serious Troubles	133
18.	We've Got This	139

About the Author 147

Praise for Pour the Wine 149

Resources 151

Discussion Guide 153

Introduction: Pour The Wine (Or A Hot Cuppa)

My cottage neighbour asked me, "So, your book, am I in your book?" We both laughed. We knew she would be. And if you have a child, or children, over 21 years of age, then yes, in some places, you will definitely see yourself. Welcome!

When friends chat, it takes only eleven minutes before the conversation turns to adult children. Yes. Just eleven minutes. "Sandy was pretty upset yesterday. Her day care sent the baby home." "The family is headed away for Christmas. Getting them organized is like pulling teeth." And on we go. Eleven minutes into a nice relaxing gathering. And someone brings up their adult kid.

There are no guidelines, no lessons, or pretty damn few, on being a parent of adult children. There is no right and wrong. Only what works for you and your family. Read on if you want help, don't need help but can take the time to enjoy some new ideas, or are just being proactive about learning what is to come as your children age.

The stories I am about to share are all real. Of course, the names have been changed to protect the innocent…and me. Some stories I took the liberty of blending with others to save time and space. To that end I also have shortened adult kids to "AKs" and also referred to them as adult children. My apologies if these stark letters, AK, do not reflect the love and care and joy you feel for your adult children. Because I love mine. I really do. I just find this period so f'ing different from what I had anticipated. It's taking a lot longer to find my footing as a parent of adults, or nearly adults. I struggle a bit to know if I've got it right.

In my life as a high school teacher, I worked with young adolescents who struggled with finding and knowing themselves, and I listened to parents who struggled to be on the side lines of this discovery period. As a life coach, I heard parents speak of the troubles they were experiencing with their older kids who were working to find a post-secondary path. And I worked alongside graduated students seeking to define and take action toward achieving their goals. These experiences alerted me to the difficult tasks involved with growth and independence in the earlier years of adulthood.

Both parents and children had struggles. But even with my varied experiences, I did not feel prepared for life with my own adult children. Children who I expected would be independent earlier, would have a design of sorts for their futures, and would have a clear awareness of self. If, with all my experience, I was in a quandary, how were other parents managing? How were they handling and living with their adult children?

My husband and I have three wonderful adult kids. And one amazing AK daughter-in-law. They will be in this book. Most of my friends and clients will be part of this book. My seventeen AK nieces and nephews will be featured. If you are in my life and you are an AK or a parent of an AK, you may see yourself right here. Please accept my appreciation for all your sharing.

These stories are about how challenging it can be to be a parent of adult kids. It demands changes in our thinking, in our behaviour, and in our expectations. It demands specific skills of some kind, I am sure. As I begin to write this book, I really don't know what skills they are! But I am up for exploring. I do know I feel compelled to drop the verb "parenting" from my vocabulary. My husband asked, over a decade ago, "When did parenting become a verb anyway?" And now, here I am, having to stop this life of "parenting" and create and evolve into some new kind of relationship with my kids, my children who are now adults.

What we like to think we did while "parenting" our children can stop now. Like disciplining. Like offering unsolicited advice or praise and offering up "participation awards." Those actions have to change if we want our children to become independently functioning and thriving adults. And I do. I believe most of us want that. We are just a bit baffled about when to let go, what to stop doing, what to start doing, and what to continue. And when. And how do they want us to be involved? Or do they?

If you are puzzled about this new stage in life, if you are a parent of one or more adult kids, this book is for you. If you believe your adult child will step into adulthood anytime soon, this book is for you, too. Pour a glass of wine or a cup of tea, sit down, and enjoy the stories, the laughter, and share tears of others who are also going through the same thing. You are not alone. We are not alone.

> "A burden shared is a burden halved."
> — **T.A. Webb, *Let's Hear It for the Boy***

Let's try and puzzle out this relationship together. Let's learn how to have an adult-to-adult relationship with our AKs.

The time for parenting has passed. Now is the time for being some other yet-to-be defined role.

I invite you to come with me on this journey. Bring your friends along. This crazy time of life is so much better when we share, sometimes with wine.

Warmly,
Gill

PART 1

Understanding the Challenge

1.
Beyond the Empty Nest

We want to celebrate! Our mission is accomplished; we've finished raising our kids. Now they are adults, grown and flown, and all the "systems" that held them to a schedule or routine are finished. Perhaps they have graduated from their schooling, an apprenticeship, or completed some post-secondary line of training. Maybe they have returned from travelling. They have physically matured and through the eyes of the world, they have flown. They are free to start a life. Our nests are empty, permanently. Or so we thought.

What Is An Adult?

As adults, our children will enter the worlds of work, relationships, financial independence, and hopefully, mature thinking. But the definition of adulthood is not clear cut. There isn't a specific line that a child glides across into formal adulthood. Adult children are post-puberty, fully developed human beings capable of reproduction. Legally, adults are over 21 years of age, or 18 years of age in some jurisdictions. However, there is a grey area when it comes to their state of mind.

Socially, intellectually, and emotionally, they can be a little incognito. Their flight into full adulthood may turn into professional changes, moves to far-off places, unemployment, blocked communications, or a lack of partners.

The world of the gig economy, digital nomads, and remote working spaces are all relatively surprising new ways of earning a living. Their world of work takes a bit of getting used to. As our AKs explore their values and their new cultures, we are taken along for the ride. My education, my world, is broadened through life with my adult kids.

My three adult kids and my daughter-in-law are very cool people. But I am confused, baffled, and ever so curious about how they make decisions, all the choices they have available to them, and the extremely broad spectrum of living these adult children experience. I think this is one of the hardest times in parenthood. And of course, the AKs are going through their own challenges, too. Big kids. Big issues. Serious problems. And so many different ways of thinking!

Our relationship with our adult children is not the same as the relationship we had with our parents. We are much more integral in our adult kids' lives. Our new relationships need creating. It is a flow, a pull and push, a true balancing act. Never static.

Flying A Little Slower

The colloquialism "times have changed" is alive and well, applicable to so many real-life situations. Scientists are studying the trends and documenting this stuff. It is not our imagination. Our children are in a very different time. I raise a glass to their strengths, determination, and ability to face these new challenges. Their stresses are real, their opportunities are varied, and the world's situation in every way is not like ours was, decades ago. Their mental health issues are increasing in number. Their relationships and expectations of us differ from what we expected from our parents.

We are not going to be the same parent we were when they were young. What kind of parent are we going to be? What do these adult kids want from us and how do we deliver? This is a new dance with them. Some fancy footwork is required, and definitely some new pattern of movement and music.

My state of confusion is not just mine. There are news articles and studies that support the fact that transition to adulthood these days offers more choices than in the past. And is on average five years longer and slower. So clearly, our journey and transition time as parents is longer and slower. The discussions with my friends and family remind me I am not alone.

My Gaggle Of Support

In my own circle of friends, I have leaned into the support I receive from a group I call my "Sisterhood of Mothers." Some are neighbours, some are gals who cottage together, others ski together, and some hold so- called *book clubs*. And oftentimes the women in each group overlap. Lucky me to be able to add seven sisters-in-law and one birth sister to this group.

In our chats, we share our fears, our worries, our chuckles, our 'WTF?' moments. Mostly, we share our stories about the uniqueness of this stage of life with our adult children. I love this generation of adult children. They give me so much to think about. And they are a constant topic of our wine chats.

Within eleven minutes the topic of conversation turns to something someone's adult child had decided, or hadn't decided, did, or didn't do. So now it is your turn to take notes at your get-togethers. How long does it take your friends to get there? Maybe they are just as baffled, confused, and surprised as I am.

> *You will teach them to fly, but they will not fly your flight. You will teach them to dream, but they will not dream your dream. You will teach them to live, but they will not live your life. Nevertheless, in every flight, in every life, in every dream, the print of the way you taught them will remain.*
>
> -Mother Teresa

2.
Research Evidence That We Are Not Alone

My daughter asked me how and where I was doing research for my book. My immediate response was, "I'm not." Admittedly pretty cocky. I had hoped to simply tell stories and relay conversations. Then I started fact-checking to see if what we were experiencing in my Sisterhood of Mothers was common and not just a local phenomenon. I went deep into the internet rabbit hole. Because learning is so fun for me, I forgot that I did not want this book to be too, well, booky.

Listening to stories is research in itself. Real moms and some dads shared stories with me. Typically, this happened while talking in a group. Usually with wine. I decided to do more research without wine and share some tidbits throughout the book. We are all pressed for time, so I'm doing you a little favour.

On a side note, sometimes my informal research was harder to obtain. Once word got out I was writing a book, my friends tried to hide. My husband is a family doctor in our small town. One day he shared this story with me: earlier that day he strolled past his waiting room and Jackie and her 23-year-old daughter, Abby, were sitting together. When the daughter came into the exam room, her mother was not with her. "Where's your mom?" my husband asked. "Isn't she coming in today?" Their usual habit was to have both in the room for the initial chat about a presenting problem. Abby was quick to respond, "Oh, she didn't come in because she doesn't want to be in Gill's book." Yes. That happens when you are researching. Your subjects get stage fright.

My research began with listening to and chatting with real parents in conversation, our wine sipping sessions. I started eavesdropping, then formally interviewing some parents, asking them what they thought. Last, I added conscious research. At first, I was shocked there was so little written about the topic. Then the teacher in me searched Google, finding various podcasts and a few book titles that interested me. I scoured Instagram accounts and read some of the few books I found. I'll share the references. And no, I will not use those pesky footnotes and I will try my best not to lecture—the references are at the end of the book. Our concerns and queries about this generation of adult children and how we transition into the new roles with them are not just ours alone. Many parents are curious. Some even research this stage of life for a living.

Who Are Our Adult Children?

Dr. Larry Nelson leads the Society for the Study of Emerging Adults, or SSEA. Any time an acronym is involved it's a little more noteworthy. I heard Dr. Nelson on the podcast called *Bite your Tongue, Building Relationships with Your Adult Children*. It's a really good podcast–great guests, scientifically based information, and solid foundational conversations. The podcast led me to the website for the Society for the

Study of Emerging Adulthood. SSEA is a multidisciplinary, international organisation with a focus on research related to emerging adulthood, defined as the age range of approximately 18 through 29 years. Real research. Pure joy for studious nerds like me.

I was surprised to learn there are professionals examining and studying this time of late teen years to 30 years of life: emerging adults, adult children, grown and flown from the nest, call them what you will. We are not alone. My Sisterhood of Mothers group is experiencing the same phenomenon as most North American parents. This period of life with emerging adults is taking longer, is going beyond 30 years, is much more complex, and is not without its trials. Research proves it, which makes it easier for me to continue the storytelling and sprinkle in some relevant, proven information we can use to learn.

"Emerging adulthood" is one term used to describe this period of development experienced by most people in their twenties in Westernized cultures, and perhaps in other parts of the world as well. It was initially defined by Jeffrey Jensen Arnett, PhD, from Clark University, in 2000. This stage of life is new to the developed parts of the world.

Emerging adulthood is typically a time of life between 18 and 29 years of age, when there is frequent change and exploration in love, work, and worldviews. Most studies conclude there is a substantial variety in young people's paths to adulthood. These years are noted as foundational to the emerging adults' flourishing or floundering in their next stage. And parents are known to be the last structure to "drop off" for the adult child's growth. Much to my surprise, we are integral in their development beyond their post-secondary education time. During this period of "emerging", adult kids experience: exploration, instability, self-focused thinking, feeling in-between, and seeing possibilities. Pause a moment. Do you recognize your adult child having those experiences? Maybe some behaviour of theirs is really a symptom of one of these feelings? Now there's some unpacking to do.

Erik Erikson, of first-year psychology class fame, speaks to the "young adult stage." This is the sixth of eight stages of psychosocial development: intimacy versus isolation. Got any memories of the lectures on this? Well, our adult kids might be in this sixth stage of psychosocial development. Note, this stage can last up to 40 years of age, so don't hold your breath. This 6th stage represents a search for intimacy that was surely further delayed during the years of the pandemic, when isolation was encouraged. Also, the plethora of social media available allows for impersonal relationships to take preference to in-person meetings and gatherings. Intimacy is harder to build these days.

Erikson noted success at this Stage 6 leads to fulfilling relationships. Struggling will lead to social isolation and loneliness. This is a stage to seek friends, lovers, and like-minded groups of people, finding their "tribe". But our developed society has put emphasis on continuing higher education or training and finding a career at this time of life. Maybe we add these pressures too. With the societal pressure to concentrate on work, and the isolation of modern-day urban living, and generally impersonal lives, the task of achieving intimacy in relationships is delayed. If our adult children find intimacy, the emerging adult gets to move into "middle adulthood". Hallelujah! There is hope.

I appreciate these groups, these authors, these podcasts. There are plenty of experts who can explain the issues around being the parents of adult children. Hearing people being vulnerable allows me some space to sit with my own thoughts. No one is without some struggles. One friend stated emphatically, "If anyone tells you their family is perfect, and without troubles, they are flat out lying." I do believe that. And my Pollyanna nature is to believe that everything will work out. Or end. But I know there has to be a process.

New Perspectives

What I most treasure about groups focused on a commonality, is that people with different perspectives on common issues challenge my way of thinking. Other women, reacting in their own way, expressing their own thoughts, make me examine how I am thinking and reacting. I am far more open when others share about their own adult kids. I can ask questions and not feel intimidated by the answers.

We have to try what fits for us in this time of being a parent to adults. For some reason, I listen wholeheartedly when I hear other parents speaking about their adult kids. I hear the ideas that come from their kids better than I hear my own. I am less attached to the answers and opinions of my friends. I have no expectations of what they might say, and I have no relationship with how they feel or what they believe. They speak, and I listen, and try to see if something new might come to me. Different perspectives and end games.

When you feel insecure, a pause does not help. A question does. Ask a question.

-Mel Robbins

Even research notes that we as parents want to be in the lives of our adult children. They want us there too. Our children do love us, says the research. But they are more concerned with battling for independence, accepting the consequences of their actions, discovering their own beliefs and values. And becoming less self-oriented. This generation is just taking more time to enter these more traditional adult roles. And delay can test our patience. Come on already. Get married, have babies, move out. In any order!

And here's a fun discovery that might help us relax. Research uncovered the fact that we are much more devoted and dedicated to our relationships with our adult children than they are concerned with us. Reread that. We are much more focused about these issues than our children. I think this is a good thing, right? Apparently, we parents have a greater "intergenerational stake". Even though adult children love their parents, parents care more than adult children do. I am reminded that our adult children are struggling too. With important things. As parents we might need to take a bit of a back seat as they focus on finding their adult selves. Their growth and change are real. To us, yes, and also to them.

PART 2

Who Are They?

3.
Their Journey to Find Themselves

There is so much to discover about our adult children. Some of our AKs are in a time of serious self-discovery. Some of them are still finding themselves, a task we feel should or might have already been accomplished. Our AKs are in a state of confusion, choices, changes, and discoveries. Still. While they are discovering, we will have to be patient to learn what they find.

Leaning Into An Identity

"Why can't they figure out what they want?" my friend Ally asked the group at our monthly book club. "They have too many choices," another friend surmised. "I don't even think my son knows who he is, let alone what he wants," mentions another. And then another states, "I don't think Shelley could do anything until she fully embraced she was gay. She didn't do that until she was 30." There was a breath of silence. Not too long, just long enough to let the gravity of that statement sink in.

Some of our adult children are still battling with or discovering their own identities. Or pushing against the opposition they might feel whether real or imagined. Shelley, our friends' daughter, had delayed being open about her homosexuality. The wine group agreed that carrying this "secret" for so long would have been really stressful. "How could she have focused on much else?" someone asks. We agreed school and work and relationships wouldn't have come easily until she lived into who she really was. Although we have a psychotherapist in our book club, we left it at that, for the time being.

One of my close friends has a daughter who has chosen to be "identified as non-binary." I had to ask a young person just how to word that. What I know is that Terry has chosen to be identified as "they/them". This is new for most of us who are parents to adults. I admire Terry's thinking and appreciate their cause and their courage. But damn it makes conversations with their mom really tough:

"We will be coming to the cottage after we collect Terry," begins Terry's mom.

"Great! You'll be here in time for dinner," I respond.

"They have to work until 5. So we'll all be in the car and leave from there."

"Oh great! You'll be here in time for dinner. Who is Terry bringing?"

"No one. Just them."

"Right. Terry and who else?"

"Just them."

"Great. See you all for dinner." I end the conversation. I don't get it. And then I do. Geez. This is not easy. Simple, but not easy.

The gender thing and adapting does not end with words or names. Heck. That is just the beginning. In my personal social circle two brave adults have transitioned. They did so with support and lots of love. They live in two different communities, in two different countries, and do not know each other. But they share a similar story. Stephen is now Stephanie. Allison is now Alex.

I wonder how long it takes a parent to adjust to that. I am only a lifelong friend, not their parent. We watched these children play and grow and giggle and cry. They were known to us with their old names: Stephen and Allie. These children, now adults, are members of our larger family communities, villages that raised our children. Villages that are changing for everyone.

Transitions For All Of Us

The transitions do not happen overnight. So much energy, concentration, therapy, and doctor time devoted to making these adult children into the people they have chosen or been born to be. Although there will be no philosophical or moral discussions here, imagine the turmoil that everyone involved would have gone through. How could a parent hold any expectations or prepare for such a turn in life?

Transitioning was complicated for all the friends of the parents. Imagine the mindset changes for the parents themselves. There has to be a real sense of loss. Sadness. All wrapped into a new contentment and pride for their child who has found themselves, who has braved the journey of recreating their social and physical being into who they know themselves to be. My experience with these adult children who have changed gender is all positive. I guess we just accept. Adjust.

Our village did. Fortunately, Steph and Al don't disown me when I slip up and call them by their old names. My own kids hit the roof and scold me openly. Like I can just undo 26 years of knowing a child. This takes time. And I will put in the effort and that time.

Conflicting Values: Love Vs. Beliefs?

I am sure there are transitioned adults who do not find themselves loved and accepted. This is just one battle that can pull families apart. A clash of morals or values. For a parent, a gender transition must be so difficult. How do you weigh your values, perhaps religion based, against your child's needs? My coaching has taught me that living your own values is one of the strongest powers we have. To disown a child or refuse to accept their change would take a firm stance, clear boundaries, and deep- rooted beliefs. Some parents and AKs are in a really, really tough place, a place which might be fraught with difference and confusion. There has to be a community to support these changes for both individuals and their parents.

At one gals' get together I explained a strategy I learned for being with an adult child who lives against their parents' values. I heard it in a podcast. If the AK and the parent want some kind of relationship, the idea is for the parent and AK to get involved in a shared activity without too much dialogue. They might see a concert together, have a game of tennis, watch a movie or a sports game, perhaps take a cooking course together. Well, that's a thought, we all agreed. "But let's not forget to share time with a therapist, too," my friend added.

Can We Be Patient?

Our adult children are still on their journey of knowing who they are. Perhaps all we can do is listen and learn. Some adult children have serious conversations going on inside. As parents we may be surprised, shocked, appalled even, at the choices they make. But this time in their life is a time of deep exploration.

I know I assumed this discovery would be complete by the time they finished school or got a job or found some life after education. Our adult children will eventually find their own comfort levels and make their own decisions. Judging them can be very dangerous and will bring rifts in the family. How we stop judging is difficult to say. Patience, for sure. Acceptance, if we want them as part of our lives. Perhaps this is a case of "you do you," and we let our adult children find how to be themselves. Our adult children are still on their journey of knowing who they are. We might want to work to listen, be curious, and learn.

Moms, It's time to let go of the dreams you had for your children.
Find out what their dreams are, and let those be your dreams now.

@never_empty_nest Instagram post

4.
What's Their Work?

Sometimes I wonder if this time is a bit awkward for me because my kids, heck most adult children these days, did not grow up and leave the nest as anticipated. Somehow, I thought all my adult kids would follow the life order: get a job, find a partner, get married, acquire a mortgage and have babies. At least have a good job by age 30. At least a job they enjoy. But that isn't how life is going for most of our grown children. Those were my expectations, though. As parents, we want a nudge to remember that our own personal beliefs, values, and history are not reason to criticise, or even question the choices our adult children make, especially about work.

This generation of our AKs and beyond, are living in a world of changed work shapes and spaces. I mean, when I was choosing a career, who knew what a graphic designer was? A data analytic scientist? A virtual assistant? An influencer? A social media manager? I doubted myself a little when I told clients or their parents that we don't really know what jobs will exist after graduation. We can hardly expect our adult kids to decide upon a career path in high school, or even in post-secondary years. Statistics and my coaching research pointed me to this truth. Secretly, I questioned it, until I just couldn't a holding pattern of some kind. Trust me. You will see a lot of circling before the landing. Suffice it to say our children aged 21 to 30 years of age, and sometimes older, are in a very unsettled time of life. Far different from when we, their parents, were their ages.

This generation of adults seems to have a slow go at finding their flight path once they leave the nest. We taught them to "fly," but we did not hand them a perfectly routed map. Nor did we offer up a distinct destination. Heck, we didn't even know the destinations available to them. We may have taught them to fly, but we have no idea where they will land!

Adjusting To Their New World

This life stage of shared confusion, choices, changes, and discoveries was the inspiration for writing this book. Never in my craziest dreams did I picture life with adult children to be such a wild ride. I envisioned them having a smooth departure from the nest and a graceful coast to the perfectly chosen landing spot. What was I thinking?

Sure, I anticipated a couple of good falls and low-impact crash landings before the final flight out of the nest. Before. But not after. And I didn't see any reason for a return trip to the empty nest for any extended period of time. Nope. I pictured a gentle upsweep as new gusts of whims and purpose gathered under their wings. And then, a gentle landing on the place where they would build their own nest.

Educational course changes and training and retraining? Yes, I expected that. As a life coach to many adult children, I know this generation has a tendency to try one path of learning and then switch to another. I did not foresee multiple anymore. Weird and unique ways of earning a living do exist. Our AKs are working and living in very different ways from us. We can accept who they are and the choices they make. Or not. One way will make our lives easier.

First Choice…Second Choice…Third Choice…

One day my friend Sandy and I were chatting about her daughter's career change from a family lawyer to interior designer, two separate university degrees, two very different career choices. Our conversation turned to my adult children, one of whom was seriously displaced by the Covid-19 pandemic.

"Maybe your son wants to be," Sandy raised her voice a little, "a digital nomad? That's a thing, right?"

"Yes, that is a big thing," I answered. I am a life coach to these nomads, and "Yes, that is the life my son is considering."

"What about Leslie?" I enquired about her lawyer-now-designer daughter. "Is she happy now that her law career has finished and she is designing and decorating homes?"

"She couldn't be happier!" was Sandy's enthusiastic response.

Work changes for these adults very quickly. My youngest was a Biochemical Engineer working in a brewery, and his next career? A high school teacher. Which took another degree. And now he is thriving. It took him a damned expensive degree and five years of work to get to where he is happiest. We celebrate his determination and search for satisfaction with his career. Many teenage students will benefit from his change to teaching. Statistics are all over the place about how many "careers" our adult children will have, with some reporting as many as 15!

Intimacy is not just about finding that "special one" who is your soulmate. There is a foundation and strength in finding a "tribe", your people. Watching my daughter find a group of caring, fun-loving friends put my mind at ease with her living a 14-hour plane flight away. She hosts Canadian Thanksgiving and her multinational gang of friends now expect the full on turkey, stuffing and sweet potatoes, and the pumpkin pies! They love her. Even without a life partner, she has found work colleagues, and super tight friendships. I am pretty sure Erik Erikson would pass her along to the next stage of psychosocial development.

And What Do They Say About Us?

Not only are there people researching the stages of emerging adulthood, there are professionals speaking to the issues that parents have during this time of their children's lives. Parents are wondering how to be. It is not only me and you. Life coaches, counsellors, therapists have set up practices to address the struggles of dealing with grown kids: entitlement, anger, feelings of abandonment, addictions, mental health issues. There are websites, Facebook pages, Instagram posts, and a plethora of resources on the internet. The health and welfare of our children affect us. As they change, we need to adapt and change too. My research has led me to follow many sources discovered on-line and listed in references at the end of the book. I listened for hours to deep conversations facilitated by host Denise Gorant of the Bite Your Tongue podcast. I ate up the information they offered on this podcast. Most books I found felt like a tough slog, and a bit more serious, or religion based than I had hoped to find.

Another statistic is that shorter stints at jobs have become the standard. Apparently, 51 percent of people now stay in any one role for *under* two year and only 30 percent of people stay in any one job for *over* four years. Job hopping is the new normal. How do we feel knowing this is the new reality? I know I am a little gob smacked but accepting. I thought it was only my kids.

The concerns around work, career, and jobs do not end at the first hiring. Society preaches to and pressures our adult children to find work/life balance, to follow their passions, to love what they do. In my experience that is not always possible and sometimes this pressure to find better balance and "fit" can lead to more anxiety. Other times, the pressure to find better leads to just that, better employment, easier work/life balance. Like the lawyer career change.

How DO You Afford To Eat?

Some adult children are making a living doing the craziest of activities, by our judgement, and we have no idea how they get paid. How does the young woman posting pictures of her recipes get money to eat? But she does. Online businesses are growing in leaps and bounds. Many adult children are working from home and selling goods online. Lots are working two or three different types of income streams. Not just one full- time and one part-time job, but selling online, building a business as a support worker, and baking cakes on the weekend. We cannot predict the futures for our adult children. Well, we cannot predict any future, but we do sometimes forget that when it comes to our own adult children.

There are people posting travel pictures, creating videos about life in tiny homes, designing video games, all earning a living. My all-time favourite? My son's friend who lives off playing poker. Yes, poker.

I met his mom at Winners. "What is Mark doing now?" I asked. "Oh, he's travelling right now and playing poker in competitions. Sounds crazy, right?" she admitted. "He loves it." "How on earth did he get into that?" I asked, always curious. "He started playing online and did really well. Then someone approached him and off he went."

I didn't know enough about this world to ask good questions. When I got home, my adult son filled me in on the details. "Remember the movie, Molly's Game?" I did. "Well, Mark is playing poker at the big tables like that, in Macau and Monte Carlo. Probably L.A., too. People call him to be at a table somewhere. When they want good competition. People will pay to get him there. Sometimes he doesn't get much sleep." There were more details, about lots of money being earned, famous people at the tables. Our adult children will do interesting "jobs" like these.

And then there is the adult child who quits one job before they have the next. "WTF?" I would share with my wine sipping friends. I do get caught up in the expectations of adult kids being responsible by my standards. Doing what is right, by my own judgement. Don't we all do that? Until we realise we are doing it?

And at the same time, I live in complete awe of what our adult children can and do achieve. Yes, our adult children will travel and change careers, they will lead a life so unlike ours, or they will get a job and stick with it and have a family and live a life in their own way. There are so many options, so many varieties of life choices. I am excited by what they find! And totally relieved I am 60 and beyond such stressful decisions.

5.
Next Chapter Love… Life

As we watch our adult children wondering and working to find their best way to make a living, they are also looking for love. This search for intimacy is most central to their development as an adult. Remember the research? In this period, dating is so perplexing. In my dating years, admittedly sounding very old, we met at a bar, or at a friend's party, or at school. Our adult kids swipe right, or swipe left, or do something with pictures. On their cell phones. So complicated to me.

"My daughter met her husband on eHarmony. It's an app." One friend was trying to teach us the benefits of online dating. "They are happily married. They enjoy all the same activities and share the love of the outdoors. Really, they are a beautiful couple. Right, Gill?" She asked for confirmation. "They sure are." I agreed. They are so good together and have so many similarities it is scary. Another friend added, "I know of two couples who met online and are married. I think those dating apps are pretty cool. Saves a lot of time. At 29, who has time to date?"

The scenarios around our AKs dating methods and choice of partners are endless: dating someone younger, dating a person their age, bringing home a pack of children along with their new partner, introducing you to their same-sex partner and announcing their homosexuality all at once. The list is full of twists and turns. The circumstances are all within the realm of what is considered healthy and normal in this time of history. Nothing is surprising, just sometimes a little baffling. Or worrisome to us older folk. Their peers don't bat an eye because every relationship is personal and an individual's choice. Live and let live, right?

Keep It Cool

As my friend Joanne reminded me, "When your kid brings home a new gal or guy, and I don't care which, don't get attached. Seriously. Don't." Break-ups and move-outs happen. You may think your Adult Kid is attached and on their way to a legal commitment, and the next thing you know they are unpacking their suitcase in their old bedroom. This is not a reason to ignore your child's partner. Just remember that living together is not necessarily a commitment for the long haul. Watch your expectations.

My good friend Ana is from Uruguay. One wine time, Ana explained to us how her 28-year-old daughter met her now spouse. As Ana told us her story and jiggled her wine glass in one hand, her gestures and thick accent took on a frightening vibration. Ana was re-enacting a moment of being very clear and straightforward with her daughter.

Ana's daughter had met a man at a fundraising event and was living with him after one month. This new beau was only three years younger than her mom, my peer! For Ana's sake I won't mention the age of either of them. But he was more than two decades older than Ana's daughter, Helena.

"I just pointed my finger at her and said, 'Here's the deal,'" Ana continued to act out her lecture: "Here's the deal," she repeated, wagging the finger of her empty hand. "There is no other way. We never, I mean never, tell your father this boyfriend's age."

Ana was telling us the history of this relationship on the same weekend she was making preparations to celebrate the visit of her first grandchild. Yup. Helena and her 55-year-old boyfriend (pretend you didn't see that number) had a son. Helena's baby father had never been married before. He was a career man. Now he was finding time to be a husband and parent.

Eventually, they did tell Helena's father. He understood. This new son-in-law just added spice to their family! And their grandson added more joy. See? It has a happy ending. Staying cool when the relationship was first announced kept the calm. Our adult children are like this. They stay calm with most kinds of relationships. It's who they are.

Flow Like Water

We certainly cannot plan or even anticipate the way our AKs will live, or the order in which they will marry, have babies, buy a house, or get a dog. Heck. I am not even sure they can plan that. It just seems to happen and unfold as it does. Why waste energy worrying and fretting? We really don't need to be taken aback that we are shocked. Initially. Very few of our adult kids are doing life as we did.

Oh heck! Let's not forget the adult children who started adult life with a child they had as a teenager, or those who get separated, divorced, remarried, are step-parents, or live in blended families. The situations for this generation of adult kids are endless. And unique. One 26-year-old I know is the stepmom to three kids, and the eldest is 15 years old. No wonder there are no guidebooks about being a parent of adult kids. There are so many different circumstances.

Get out of the seriousness of the things we cannot control.
-My yoga instructor

    The flow and order of major life events, as we have known them, are no longer set in stone. Relationships are so complicated. Why would a parent even ask an adult child about their choices? Our children will date, whatever that looks like, have sex, maybe have a baby, maybe get married, maybe move in together, and of course, buy a dog. What order they choose will be a mystery. What age, gender, marriage status, family situation will also be what it is. And there is nothing we can do except, dare I say it, accept their lives and their boundaries, if we want a relationship with our adult kids. Learn to zip it sometimes. Look at the long game. I assume you do want a relationship with your adult child, given you are reading this book.

    Lives have been interrupted by changes in school and course choices, addictions, illnesses, living with a partner, then finding a different partner, and even more impactful, finding a new gender. Living together is more the norm. Having roommates who come and go is financially more viable. There is no pattern, no norm. Their hearts will be broken. Our hearts will be broken. With some AKs, time and time again, they will struggle, we will struggle.

We Want The Best…But Maybe Don't Know Best

So how can we support them without being a part of their issue? What can we do to rest easy, be less surprised, and allow our children to live their own lives? These are the questions we try to answer as we pour our wine and chat about life with AKs.

Sitting at my friend's place for a card game, the topic turned to our openness for inclusion in our families. I told the story of one young woman, who we all knew, from an East Indian family. "Aesha told me she was allowed to date anyone she wanted. But she was expected to marry an East Indian. Probably someone she met through her friends or her parents' friends."

"No way," my girlfriend reacts mildly shocked.

"Yup, I believe that," says another.

"Did you notice what happened with the Taher family? All three kids have married Arab Muslims. They travelled the world, lived in cities all across Canada, and still ended up with an Arab Muslim spouse. How does that happen?"

"Well, you can fall in love with anyone anywhere, might as well make it easier on yourself," chimed in another.

Part of me cannot even believe we are even having this conversation for crying out loud; it is 2024! I sit up closer to the edge of my chair. The curious part of me is excited to hear where this conversation will go. I am sadly disappointed.

"Studies have always shown that marriages last longer when there are more socio-economic and cultural similarities. Less to fight about."

"Well, we do want happy kids, right?"

How can I argue with that? I was just hoping for a little deeper discussion. My AKs would have jumped all over us even noticing (and commenting on) these "dated'" observations. But we do pass judgement and wonder. In our own little circles, we worry about the partners our children choose. Come on. We all want our adult children to find the right partner, if they are choosing one.

Parents always want the best for their children. And we think we know what defines "best." In the Facebook posts of groups of parents of adult children, one of the most noted complaints is the effect the partner has on their child. It could be the partner who "took my daughter away from me and banned me from seeing my grandchildren." You get the idea. These partners can be the cause of many family distresses. These partners often bear the blame for the adult child's behaviour. Our adult children are coming home with partners of various genders, diverse cultures, and big age gaps. Not all of us are happy about this. But at what cost do we argue?

One of our family's younger friends has transitioned from a female to a male. She was dating a female, as a female, and they continued their relationship through the physical transition. Today they are a happily married couple, visibly identified as "he" and "she." Such strength and support for one another. Not easy on the parents of the couple either. I admire them all. Their actions have stood for love and patience and acceptance.

I ask myself, when faced with unique circumstances within a couple's lives: "What difference does it make to anyone else, but them? If the couple is happy, no one is being harmed, and both are supportive of one another; what is the problem?" Is this a time to bite your tongue? Zip it? It's not morally or physically dangerous for them. But does it seem morally or physically dangerous to us, the parents? Are we caught up in our personal loss that our expectations were not met, or our values are not being lived through our adult children? These are tough questions.

This is the point, isn't it? We might judge their choices in the name of their protection or our values. Sometimes, almost all the time, we just have to live with the knowledge there is nothing we can do. Even if an adult child is in an abusive situation, and they do not want to leave, there is nothing we can do. The police won't even press charges in an abuse situation without the victim's consent. So how can we affect the situation?

Another tough question: how do we know our adult kids have made a commitment to stay together in life? Is it when they tell us they are expecting? A baby. Not a rescue dog. Or wait…are they committed to one another when they get a dog together? "They have been living together for eight years. Do you think that means they are planning to stay together?" my cousin asked about her son and girlfriend. "He tells me he is going to propose, but Christmas came and went, and then Valentine's Day. I don't get it." And that's just it, right? We don't get it. But do we need to?

And then, when our adult kids do get married, what a variety of services, ceremonies, celebrations, and choices. Some of these weddings are totally over the top. Six to eight attendants, each. Two cute ring bearers and a field full of flowers. Or none. A friend gets ordained, and they run off to a mountain-fed lake for a camping wedding weekend. Just six people. How romantic. That was my son and his wife when Covid-19 changed the course of their planned 235-person-guest-list wedding. From one extreme to the other. Don't worry, though. Six weeks before the second official celebration date they flipped the wedding location to the other side of the Canada-U.S. border and went ahead with a banger of a celebration. Smaller guest list. Only 130 people, only. Another best friend officiated! Gotta love those online officiant courses. And the variety of weddings we may be blessed to attend. Yes. Adult children do these sorts of things.

And after the wedding, comes the honeymoon. Or after the children. Usually after something or other, it seems. "Brad and Olivia are pregnant, so they are having a honeymoon when the baby is old enough to stay with us," our bridge-playing friend told the table of gals. "Who decides when the baby is old enough to stay with you?" a smart alec asked. We laughed. "Are Brad and Olivia married?" is the next question. "Yes. Last summer they flew to Portugal and were married out on a rock. It was them and their photographer. They went to City Hall first, for the legal thing. I'm pretty sure they said vows on the rock, so that was where they had their wedding picture." "Wasn't that trip called a honeymoon?" is the obvious question asked. And we circled back to the initial declaration. "No. Because they are going on their honeymoon after the baby is old enough to stay with us."

A gaggle of giggles. And a sip of wine.

The moment we realise that how we react to our kids' behaviour has more to do with how we're feeling than what our kids are doing, is the moment we understand that our main job as parents must be to keep ourselves emotionally healthy.

-@respectfulmom Instagram

Expect The Unexpected

We have to look after ourselves. These surprises are merely unexpected blessings, right? Our adult children are doing as they please. Most do just what makes them happy. That's exactly what I have always hoped for my children. If I had set expectations around what I wanted for my adult kids, I am not even sure what I might have imagined. I am confident I hoped and still hope they would find special intimate relationships because I so value connection and love. Loneliness is not something I want anyone to experience. That's just me.

And that is why we need to look after ourselves and know ourselves. Which could be an entire book! See that therapist or coach, do yoga, meditate, find a hobby. Do what it takes to make our own lives full of happiness. How frightening it would be for everyone if the happiness of a parent was dependent solely on the choices of their adult children.

6.

Not All Nests Are Empty

My last holiday was luxurious. One afternoon I found time to fill my beach bag with a pop, a towel, and a shiny, brand-new magazine. Lowering myself onto a poolside lounger, I slipped on my sunglasses and excitedly opened the fall edition of Real Simple. The magazine didn't appear to be one that would include inspiration for my writings. I bought it for decorating ideas. Yet, there it was, an entire article on multi-generational households. The title was "All Together Now," by Amy Maclin.

Yup. We had hoped our adult children would have jobs and love, and a place of their own. Yet, a lot of my friends have their adult kids coming back home after a year or two away. Some have adult kids who have never left. Our empty nests aren't being emptied for long.

According to the magazine article's author, "North Americans have not lived in multi-generational housing for the past 50 years." Factually, this moving home thing and living together as adults is a bit different for us. But, as the world is today, some adult children have had no option but to return to the family home. And there are lots of other variations of living together. All surprising to me. Seemingly acceptable to others.

They Never Left

Our town is fortunate to have both a community college and a university. Many graduating high school students stay right at home to pursue their education. "Why wouldn't I stay here and live at home?" a coaching client asked me. We were working together to build an education plan. "It's cheaper. And I can get my laundry done, meals prepped, and have a car to use." Staying put for the four-year degree just made perfect sense to her. And two years post-graduation, she is there, sleeping in her own childhood bedroom. "What is going to give her incentive to move out?" her Mom asked me. We giggled when a friend mentioned the movie Failure To Launch. "Are you going to hire a boyfriend?" she asked. Eventually she will leave we all agree. "Or I will," says her Mom.

In daily chit-chat, it seems my friends have not had serious issues with their adult children who have come to share their homes. But after a few glasses of wine, more truths are shared. They have frustrations with adult kids who do not contribute to their own personal expenses. I laughed when I listened to a story about a son who puffed out his chest and told his mom, "My 30 hours a week covers everything I need. I work to live. I do not live to work." Work/life balance is important to this generation. Mom did have to ask, "Is your internet and television part of your living? How about the roof over your head? Because I'm paying those bills." As the son walked away he muttered, "You've never complained about that before." Clearly they didn't have any discussions around financial expectations when the son moved back home.

Who's Movin' Who?

Susan's son just returned home from travel and brought a new woman with him. Susan doesn't have big complaints, but the day-to-day dynamic of the house has changed: "My son's girlfriend has decided she controls the TV channels every night after 9 p.m." Susan was just venting a little before a card game, with wine in hand. "I go out for my evening walk and when I come home, the girlfriend is sprawled on the couch with the TV remote in her hand! She has the nerve to tell me she is so happy we have a TV in our bedroom. 'I just don't know how I could get to sleep without seeing the nightly news,' she tells me."

The girls at the wine table have questions: "Did you tell her that you don't want to watch TV in your bedroom?" "How about you ask her to go to the basement to watch the TV down there?" "Can't you ask your son to tell her to use the other TV at night?" We all had some questions to ask, but no one had the answer about how to resolve the issue. Until Nikki asked: "When they moved in, did you have some kind of 'round table' discussion about living together? I heard that a meeting like that can be really helpful."

And so our wine-induced conversation turns to how to start and manage a "round table" discussion about living together, before the next gen moves in and things get crazy. Brilliant idea. And we even decided it's okay to have the meetings on a regular basis. Just to keep everyone respectful of one another. Someone mentioned she wished she had done this every spring before the kids moved back for the summer. "That might have saved us some fighting during those university years." Maybe this is what the experts are referring to when they discuss setting boundaries.

Our Adult Kids are learning about setting boundaries also. You will not be sounding foreign to them if you venture into a family meeting about healthy boundaries. Similar to rule making, boundary setting is there for the good of everyone. Boundaries such as: *Speak to one another with respect. Attend to your private belongings in common spaces. Be home by 2 a.m. or call.* Just entering into such family round table discussions might open the space for clear communication.

Such a shame that there are families in living situations that are so disruptive. Preventative meetings, setting boundaries: such sanity-saving ideas. And there are many other articles out there to assist with such meetings. I googled that, too. This is one example of why we, the wine sippers, believe we are capable of running the country.

Jo and Steve have their eldest daughter, Nicole, and her boyfriend living in their house. They have been there for over a year. I don't know if it was planned, or discussed, or they just woke up one day and David had moved in. The four of them have found their own rhythm. They just work. For the most part. The typical complaint of dishes left unwashed is shared with the wine pals.

I asked Steve if the kids were house hunting. He told me, "When Jo and I were house hunting, we looked at around fifty houses before we felt we could buy. These two are not even looking. Maybe we're too accommodating?" During a later conversation, Nicole and her boyfriend mentioned they hoped to be out of the house within the next three months. Steve and I exchanged a look and stifled a laugh. And guess what? They did it!

Keep The Doors Open

This is what I'm talkin' 'bout. The surprises of being a parent to young adults. The parts of life with them that we did not see coming. How do we deal with this change in life and living? How do we continue our relationships when not only are our own children under our roof, but their significant other, children, and pets are also? Are we moms, or friends, or in-laws, or what? Not that we need to have a title, just a guideline of how we are supposed to behave and react, and what expectations we can voice.

One friend's daughter just moved back home with her 4-year-old and 8-month-old sons. My friend and her husband are thrilled. Of course, they are not happy about their son-in-law not being there, but they are supporting the separation decision made by the adult kids, by just being there for their daughter and grandsons. My friend told me she wants to be supportive and has discussed with her daughter that she shouldn't bad mouth the boys' dad. "Was that crossing the line?" I asked her. She told me she wasn't sure, but her daughter was appreciative and agreed.

In another friend group, a young woman is living with her fiance and his parents. She and her fiance have one son. Marriage is not in their immediate plans, but one day. They are not always happy about the arrangement, but they have little choice. Housing is so expensive and both have seasonal work. They are happy to give his parents a bit of money and hope to have the parent's mortgage paid off more easily. A win-win situation.

Some of my friends are switching things up. They aren't waiting for their retirement or urgent healthcare needs to move in with their own adult children. Selling the family home might be the best financial or comfort driven decision. Apparently, this movement is known as the reverse-boomerang effect. The move seems to be driven by changing attitudes about family life, the high cost of housing, and serious challenges in finding reasonably priced childcare services. Regardless of the reason, adult children and their parents are living together. And living together as adults brings its own relationship issues.

So how do we cope with living together with adult children? How do our adult kids cope? In my life coaching practice, I learn from both sides: the parents and the adult children. There are complaints, and whining, and then there are laughs and joy and lots of loving moments. I hear of both ups and downs. But there are plenty of scenarios where families find only troubles, problems, and fights.

For now, we could consider that adult children and their parents need to stay in full communication before they go back to living together. That most civil idea about the round table discussion seems quite brilliant. There could be talk about how to behave toward one another, how to show respect for one another, how to manage their new relationship boundaries: chores, money, space use, parking, and car use. Simple, but not easy. All parties have to respect the will to be a family, to cohabitate again, although in a newer form.

And parents will pour the wine and chat with our friends who will remind us that we have to design the relationship we want with our AKs, especially if they are back under our roof.

Or we are under theirs. What suits one of us does not suit us all. What one of us will tolerate, another will not. And we will remind each other, when the going gets too tough, that we'll need to reach out for professional help and build our village of assistance. While the adult children are living their lives, most parents are still eager to be a healthy family unit.

PART 3

Who Are WE?

7.
You're Seeing Who?

Life together, as "we" parents and adult children, isn't always easy. With turmoil in one stage of my own adult life, I decided to go see a psychotherapist. "That's good," my daughter told me. "I meet with mine regularly at times, and often check in monthly." My youngest reminded me, "You know Mom, lots of people see therapists."

Geez, "lots of people" do. I get that. My generation just doesn't tell everyone! It is not that out there. When I confided to a friend that I'd been seeing a therapist, she casually responded, "Oh, is it Winny? Isn't she wonderful? My kids and I have used her throughout the years." Hmmm. Take that.

> *Remember as far as anyone knows, we're a nice normal family*
>
>   -Sign in the front hall, gifted to us by my sister-in-law

Our adult children are seeking help to keep their brains and their thinking healthy. They see the same alarming rates of suicide, depression, and anxiety we do. Their peers are hurting. We live in stressful times. And many adult kids do not find us, the parents, blameless.

I am just learning I've inflicted lots of trauma on my kids. Take note, our traditional definition of trauma is not how trauma is viewed today. I will not go into that here. Be careful how you use that word. You can google all you want and find reputable information. For our purposes, I'm using the definition that we may have, as parents, brought about some memories for our children which have had very disturbing long-term emotional effects. And I do not take that lightly. I did. I am sure both my husband and I did. We just had no clue. And now we do not want to repeat any such event. This quote of Maya Angelou sums up our thinking:

Do the best you can until you know better. Then when you know better, do better.

-Maya Angelou

Never, ever, did I think my kids would be seated in front of a psychotherapist, as adults, talking about their parents, their childhoods, their sibling rivalry. Feeling traumatised about what we had done or failed to provide. And paying good money for the professional service!

Okay, one child WAS conceived post vasectomy. My daughter asks, "Can we still call it a vasectomy when it didn't work?" Hmmm. Maybe *that* had an effect on our youngest's emotions, his feelings of belonging. Maybe that knowledge has brought him to therapy. Maybe.

Good Intentions And Worry

Our whole family did go to a therapist when there were troubles adjusting to our move across the ocean. We took our kids away from Canada when they were eight, seven, and three years of age. Our intentions were to stay two years in Riyadh, Saudi Arabia, and we stayed for six years. Our eldest had the most difficulty leaving behind all his eight-year-old friends, his teammates, his walkable neighbourhood, close family members, and daily culture.

Yes. We did *that* to our children. Never intending to invoke any harm. And the end result seemed to be: they loved it, got a valued education, wished we had stayed longer, and learned to travel the world independently, without anxiety. One child even moved back to the Middle East. The trips to the family therapist seemed to be worth it for them and us. But seeing a therapist now? As adults? And encouraging me to join them? The world has changed.

And aren't we all thankful for that? This generation of 25-to-40- year-olds understands the power of thinking. For all their mental health issues, there is a positive: our adult children are working to destigmatize therapy. They have learned about the wild rides our minds will take us on unless we take the reins. The power of emotions is real for them. And they are open to the possibilities that our thoughts and beliefs can be changed for an overall healthier life. This generation is open to new ways of perceiving their world, and know they better be open because their world is changing, all the time.

Just this week I was reminded by my 34-year-old adult child, "Brain work is hard work." Our adult children know mental health is serious stuff. If they don't grow their understanding of their thinking and beliefs, they will be left behind. Or depressed, sad, and lonely. So, I see my therapist. And they see theirs. And we talk about it.

In this changing world, we have to acknowledge the AKs' perseverance and acceptance. I feel relieved I am over 60 and not just beginning my adult life. It is tough out there. Jobs, wages, inflation, suicides, and drug abuse all feature in news headlines regularly. This generation is experiencing higher levels of stress, anxiety, and depression. There are record numbers of deaths of despair. Many parents are watching their Adult Children, and some even younger children, facing addictions of all sorts. The isolation from the pandemic has wreaked havoc with the human spirit and our need to be social animals.

This is why as a parent of adults, I worry. There is a lot of "bad" going on out there. I do want to be sure they are well and flourishing, without being interfering or overbearing. Therein lies the quandary. When do we step in and when do we butt out? We revisit this question so often over our glasses of wine.

How To Parent Through Crisis

A long-time friend confided in me that her daughter, at the age of 20, had experienced addiction. I knew her child had been asked to leave a private school and rumours circulated around town as to why. My friend was at the breaking point when she decided to call a local doctor friend and have him converse with her adult daughter. At two in the morning. While her daughter was coming down from a violent, drunken episode. That took guts. And vulnerability. It was time to intervene.

Fortunately, her daughter agreed to go into a treatment facility. Throughout the period of recovery, my friend attended all the mandatory family meetings and worked at listening to and fully understanding her AK. From a parent's perspective, there was a problem and she bravely reached out to find a solution they could both accept. Clearly the adult child had to make the commitment. Their relationship is strong now. I think listening and understanding were the healing forces.

On a warm summer night another friend, a local high school guidance counsellor, shared some of her troublesome times with her own adult child who was experiencing anxiety. The stress was so severe, their adult child had quit school and come home to isolate themselves. She told me her son chooses to smoke marijuana to relieve their troubles and quiet their mind; they see a therapist, too.

She shared with me, "With all the kids I have taught, all the students who used me as their guidance counsellor, I have had no conversation as difficult as the ones I am having with my own adult child. This is the hardest relationship to build, ever."

She continued to explain that her AK opened up to her, saying, "Mom, you never validate anyone's feelings. You jump in to solve the issue or tell them that everything will be alright. How about just letting them sit in their emotions for a bit? What about just letting them feel for a while? Acknowledge them. The struggles they feel." The son even went on to give a specific example.

My friend was crushed. She understood what she was hearing. As a guidance counsellor, she would listen but as a parent she admittedly rushed in to solve problems, make it all better, help the pain to go away. That's not always what our adult kids want or need. We both agreed. Our AKs can be so emotionally intelligent. And even better, they know what emotional intelligence is.

Our adult kids get this mental health thing. Lots of parents are quick to find solutions, fast to comfort with options, and placate with alternatives and encouragement to look for the silver lining. Admittedly that's where I hang. Always looking to find the silver lining, to see the positives. The Pollyannas of the world understand this request to just listen. Let's just allow our adult kids to sit with us and their emotions for a bit. Research shows there is good in feeling the bad. Believe me, I checked out all the emotional intelligence materials. All agree. Feel the feels. Bad and good. Perhaps we don't always slow down long enough to just hear the pain, the hurt, the frustration. Maybe we do offer advice too quickly. Our adult children seek validation. We all do.

Now there's a new skill to learn as a parent of AKs: how to stop parenting our adult kids; how to listen without offering a list of "try this" or "why don't you do that?" Our family is a support network and we can strengthen our bonds with understanding and caring. And acceptance.

> *"Most people do not listen with the intent to understand; they listen with the intent to reply."*
>
> Stephen Covey

8.

French Tucks and Other Lessons

If we stay open to them, our adult children will keep us involved in the world that is around us today. We will stay younger if we keep learning and listening and being curious. Research backs this up. And our adult kids have lots to teach us. And they do not hold back.

Fall nights at the cottage are my favourite. I get to snuggle into something a bit cozier. One night, a couple of years ago, I thought I was looking pretty good in my long-sleeved pale blue 'jean' shirt, paired with straight legged dark blue jeans. But not quite. The girls on the veranda of our cottage, grown adult kids, cousins and siblings, had something to say about my attire.

"That looks nice, Aunt Gill. Want me to show you how to do a 'french tuck'?"

"Sure?" I was hesitant. "What's a french tuck?"

And so my lesson began.

My sister-in-law, who worked for decades as a fashion buyer for the clothing store Town and Country, agreed I was 'rockin' the french tuck. But even she is not spared fashion support from her adult daughters. "The girls are taking me shopping tomorrow. Apparently I have forgotten how to buy clothes for myself. And they told me that."

Our daughters offer these kind pieces of advice. We like to look good and we trust their tastes, so we comply. We shop with them. We buy our clothes with them. Our credit cards are at-the-ready. Usually a gift or two is purchased along the way. For them, the daughters. Smart girls!

As much as my adult children puzzle me, they bring the gift of new information into my life. They have opened the doors of self-development, social media, computer living, great music, and fun fashions. Their moves have taken me to places on this planet I would not likely have explored. My list of people I call 'friends' has blossomed to include their friends, and parents of their friends.

Mona, nearing retirement, renovated her basement to make a second income with rentals. This decision was at the suggestion and encouragement of her adult children. She and her husband didn't want someone there all the time so her adult kids suggested the renovation be for a short-term rental. "You know Mom, a place on Airbnb. It's a great way to have a secondary income as you enter your retirement years," her son told her. "The basement will be a great short-term rental for now, and maybe in your later years, you'll want someone to live there full time. You know, another set of ears and eyes on you as you age." Gee thanks. "And when we come to visit, we can stay there."

Mona is loving this income and really enjoys meeting her guests. The adult children were right. And they also pitched in to finish the reno and make the website live. That is a special relationship of teaching. Both parties get bonuses.

Changing worlds are less daunting because our adult children are there to teach us. And remind us. And suggest to us. And tell us exactly what we are doing wrong and how to correct it. Oh, they also feel comfortable enough to explain exactly what we did wrong in our parenting methods. How we could have offered more discipline, or less. I forget. It depends which AK is talking.

Yes, our adult kids have opinions. As well as many ideas and much information. And they are not afraid to share it all with us. Some of their lessons have been so valued by me. I know my way around online banking and love making deposits and payments from my phone. So tech savvy now. And I learned how to "cast" to my television screen from my phone or computer. Not sure I said that right, but it works. Netflix and Youtube and all those other fun programs are second nature to me now. Thank goodness for adult kids. They are so smart! And we have to be smart too because our adult children do not have self-imposed boundaries around what they say to us. Their lectures and opinions can be endless.

The Lecturer

One summer night the dishes were on the table awaiting clearing. We had just finished dinner at my cousin's house. Three couples and one adult child. Dinner was done and still we sat chatting. The empty wine bottles multiplied. The table seemed quite cluttered, although the dishes were gone. The conversation abruptly changed. My adult niece witnessed an open eyeball glare my sister gave to her husband as he brought yet another bottle of red wine to the table.

Our conversation was interrupted by a lecture. The 'lecturer' was the sole adult kid at the table. "Mom," she began, as she stood, about to reach for the new bottle. "We are all concerned about Dad's health, right? (pause and a glance toward her mom) I am with you on that." She formed a heart shape with her thumbs and forefingers and brought it to her own anatomical heart area.

"But. I am with Dad when it comes to the wine issue." My niece expertly wielded the corkscrew to open the bottle. "Dad and I are together on this. Don't try and curtail our wine drinking. You're being ridiculous."

Her mom just shrugged and exchanged knowing glances around the table. I am pretty sure I have also been the accused. Once or twice.

Our adult children feel quite comfortable challenging our ways and decisions. They have little hesitation in stating their viewpoint, anywhere. I do admire their push to keep us healthy. After all, they do feel some responsibility for caring for us as we age. Sometimes, their ideas of caring for us can become a little too invasive. Believing they are permitted and in fact, authorised, expected, and maybe privileged to make comments about our behaviour. Over the top? Perhaps. Borderline 'entitled'? Suggested by some.

Definitions from Oxford Languages
en·ti·tled
adjective
believing oneself to be inherently deserving of privileges or special treatment.
"kids who feel so entitled and think the world will revolve around them"

I remember coming to my parent's home for a visit and I would walk down the back hall and lower the temperature on the thermostat a couple of degrees. Typically I would hear my Dad, "Hey Gill, you don't live here anymore. We regulate our temperature." It seemed pretty logical when he stated that. I would return the house to their chosen temperature. Our adult kids are not likely to change because we suggest they might, and often, we don't feel that we can say anything to them. We might just walk on eggshells so as not to ruffle feathers. Why is that? What do we fear? There is a suggestion that we want to be 'liked' by our adult kids, so we appease them. Hmm. I wonder.

My friend, Gail, had a good story about the arrogance, or entitlement, our adult kids can have. "Did I tell you our niece came to the cottage for a weekend and rearranged the furniture?" Her story began. "She what? WTF? Oh, come on." Various responses from around the table.

"Yup. She moved all the living room furniture when she arrived on Friday," Gail spread her arms wide, "and then went home on Sunday." Her arms dropped to her lap. "With her two cats that she takes everywhere." "Wait a minute," Sally interrupted, "your family has severe cat allergies!"

Gail and her two siblings share their childhood cottage. Their parents are still alive, but not physically able to visit the cottage. Now there are 10 grandchildren sharing the cottage with them. And four spouses. The cottage furniture has been in the same place for over 50 years. Gail's niece decided the cottage needed a change. So she just moved the living room furniture. No asking, no discussion, she just up and moved it.

"And she brings her cats into the bedroom she claims. The largest bedroom, because she 'got there first.'" Gail added.

What do you do with that? Given that the furniture mover is the child of Gail's brother, the friends at the table agreed he might speak with his own daughter. To avoid further design changes. Perhaps talk about cat allergies, too. Or should Aunt Gail, herself, open the conversation? "No way," Gail interrupts. "I am already Bitch Aunt Gail." So who talks to the furniture mover? Or do you just move the furniture back and let it go? Don't ask me! I have no f'ing idea. Wait. This might be just the time for boundaries.

I do know these are the sorts of issues we face now. Do I think for one minute as a young woman I would have been a furniture mover? Absolutely not. I would stick to temperature settings. But these are the days we live in. We can accept that or live with the consequences of walking on eggshells, or addressing the elephant in the room. Pick one. Gail and her immediate family were the last to leave the cottage that weekend. They chose to return the furniture to its original placement. I can't wait to hear the outcome! Pour more wine.

Agency

These are instances where we might ask ourselves: Do I have to listen to this, or put up with such behaviour? Or can we decide, we don't have to take this? Not from our adult kid. Why should we compromise our own ability to voice an opinion? Don't our kids owe it to us to listen to our ideas, our advice? Interesting dilemma. What are our choices? Zip it. Button it. Shut up. Offer love. Offer encouraging words. Build their confidence. Set boundaries. Save ourselves. Save the relationship. Lots of choices. And quite a balancing act.

Our adult children want agency in their own lives. And as we continue to be their parents, our listening, and not arguing, is one way to keep the respect and relationship alive. As much as it may hurt us to remain unheard, our ego can survive being second. Most days. Right? And can we enter into conversations around boundaries, what is acceptable and what is rude, mean, or uncalled for? Again, solid communication seems the answer.

Our adult kids have opinions and many ideas. Lots of them. They want us to be up-to-date and current in our knowledge and our thinking. They want us to be healthy and happy. Sometimes, they might overstep their boundaries. And perhaps there are times adult kids don't give us credit for what we do know. Again, this balance is tough to establish. What do we have to offer, and what do the adult kids have to contribute? What can they teach us without us getting defensive? How can we and they offer suggestions without being opinionated and critical?

These are the balances we seek. Our adult kids have the 'smarts' for managing this world. I can't count the times I am thankful that I am in the later decades of my life, and not starting out in today's world. The world in which they live is new to me. I let them vent a bit and teach me new skills, new ways of being. And I am learning to listen without judgement. Believe me, this is a lesson in progress!

9.

Sibling Rivalry

He's always been your favourite. You and Dad both spoil him! The whole family bends over backwards to make him happy. It isn't fair.

Sounds like a ten-year-old chirping at their parents, right? It wasn't. Those words were spoken by an adult kid. A fully grown adult. Sibling rivalry never dies. Be prepared. This is another one of the surprises I have with adult children. Aren't they over this? My brother-in-law asked, "Will this be going on when they get to retirement?" We laughed and agreed the kids will still be arguing over our wills. This is what family does.

As parents of AKs we know that each child has different needs. We don't treat each of our kids the same. Heck, we were not the same parents to each of them as they were growing up. What we learned between the first child, second, third and so on…made us different people, with changed perspectives. Admittedly, what the youngest was permitted to do, the first born was absolutely not. And yes, the curfew times got later, the TV watching was less monitored, the car was more available for the youngest.

Our kids actually did not have the same requests of us. One wanted to play guitar, another wanted to go to Mexico for spring break, one just wanted a bedroom painted. We can identify the obvious differences, but I bet there were subtle differences around how we treated each child. So no, we were not the same parents to each of our children. And yes, there may be a perception that one kid got more than the other or others. No family is exempt from these feelings.

Different Kids, Different Relationships

So how are we expected to have the same relationship with each child when even now, as adults, they do not have the same requests or demands of us? One AK may want to see us regularly and live close by. Another might live miles and miles away and really just hopes we might visit for one weekend, or lucky us, even two weekends a year. And then, of course, one may want their parents to come very seldom or even not at all.

Families are like this. AKs have different needs. Each child has developed their own relationships with us. And still, they may believe another sibling is the favourite, getting more, being "spoiled." Some adult children openly claim they are indeed the favourite, the only daughter, the youngest son, the prized first born, and they may just out and out ask for more. More time. More money. More attention.

And then there are situations when it is just easier to be with one adult kid more than another. My friend has a daughter, Emma, who lives in town, so she sees Emma or speaks to Emma, almost daily. Her eldest daughter, Sally, lives four hours away. And probably doesn't want to see her mom or speak to her mom daily. Mom and Sally have butted heads pretty much as long as I have known them, at least 25 years! I admit, I tittered a little when my friend wondered why it was that Sally never sent her pictures of her firstborn daughter. I have an Instagram account and I am 'friends' with Sally. Sally posts pictures of her daughter regularly. I love watching my friend's granddaughter grow! My friend told me, "I asked Sally why I didn't get regular pictures and Sally told me she posts almost daily on Instagram." "So get an Instagram account," I suggested. My friend simply made a "harumph" sound. "I have no idea why I should get an Instagram account to see pictures of my own granddaughter," she said. I giggled.

Sorry.

Each of our AKs have different asks of us. And most AKs who live in their parents' town will get more time, attention, and gifts. It is just logistically easier. But who gets their cell phone bill paid because they are on a family plan? Who gets to share the Netflix account? Discussions around financial agreements such as cell, TV, and even car insurance, are often fuel for sibling rivalry. And how do we as parents explain treating one bill differently than the next? And how do we decide when these arrangements end? I have no idea. It is tough to justify, really.

Show Me The Money

My friends sometimes chat about the question of financial gifts: do we give each child the same, whether they need it or not? Or do we give to each according to their needs? One friend keeps track of every dollar loaned or gifted to each child and balances the sums for future reference. What references? When? In the will? Do shared vacations and cell phone bills get tallied? Do you count babysitting hours? I wonder.

Parents who want to keep their relationships strong with each of their AKs have these conversations amongst themselves. How do we balance giving and sharing without upsetting the others? How much do we tell each sibling about what we give to, or do for, the others? Does the whole family need to know when a loan is made? If one AK can't come on the holiday, do they still get the money paid for the family flight or accommodation? Geez. It can get complicated. And no one likes to keep secrets, do they?

One Christmas, Jane's family was hosting only two of their three adult children. The other AK was heading to their in-laws, who live two hours away from Jane's home. On their way to that city they drive right by Jane's house. Her daughter suggested that perhaps on the way to her in-laws they could stop in and pick up their Christmas stockings. Her daughter was talking about the filled-with-goodies, personally hand-stitched by Jane, Christmas stockings. Jane is the absolute best stocking stuffer!

Well, this situation brought on a multi-generational dinner table squabble. Jane and her husband had different opinions. Jane thought, "Why should they get to be a part of the family tradition of our great stockings when they aren't with us?" Rob disagreed. "We want them to enjoy Christmas and those stockings are a part of that." Even Jane's mother got in on the conversation. Grandma voiced, "Those stockings are a part of Jane's tradition. It is Jane's thing to share." Jane's other adult kids chimed in, "No way. If you're not here, you're not here. No stockings." Wouldn't it have been fun to be a fly on that wall? These are issues we have with our AKs. Maybe not particularly Christmas stockings, but similar. In every family there is something to bicker over. Right?

My AKs playfully chat about bigger 'gifts' like "Who gets the cottage?" and "Who gets the house?" I know if it came down to our end of life and a decision was made in favour of one child, a fight would break out. My husband and I decided we had better have a well written, very detailed will. And the lawyer suggested we sell absolutely everything as we age and avoid any arguing. Create a common enemy. Us. There are books written on these topics and experts on family law. Just more to research. More to think about. Just another moment of stress for parents of AKs. Sibling rivalry? Who would have thought we would be discussing this as parents of adults? Yet families divide over such jealousy.

They've Always Had Different Parents

> *My sister and I never engaged in sibling rivalry. Our parents weren't that crazy about either one of us.*
>
> -Erma Bombeck

A colleague and I were discussing sibling rivalry and realised that we actually are not the same parent, or even the same adult person with each of our children. Our eldest child was our treasured, mystifying firstborn. I often laughed about whether we could send them back because we probably inflicted the most trauma on them as we were just learning the whole game, and quite anxious with most events. I have been told that with each subsequent child, parents become more and more lax and relaxed. My story to illustrate that is a family favourite. I left my youngest son at day care after I finished my teaching day. My lesson plans were packed up, I got in the car, and went home. Not once did I leave him behind, but twice.

Our daycare was a 25-minute drive away and I couldn't drive (we lived in Saudi Arabia) so both times I had to get a driver to get me back to the daycare and home again. Sorry, son. Clearly I had something else on my mind. Twice. We all know I never would have done that with our first child. No way.

Other generations had much larger families than we do now. My husband, number eight of nine, recalls being left at camp one year. When the counsellors phoned his mom, she told them he would have to stay another night as the drive was six hours to get him. She would come the next day. My husband stayed at his camp counselor's home for the night. He was 8 years old! And that is what parents do. Juggle according to their abilities. Maybe that is why families are getting smaller.

As parents we change, we grow, we relax. And so, yes, we will be different, and perhaps not consistent. Perhaps our changed treatment of siblings can be frustrating, or envied. But is that cause for our AKs to fight, to bicker, to name call? Imagine a 30-year-old claiming their sister was the favourite child. All my nieces and nephews, except for the only child family, tell me they have scolded their parents for picking a favourite child. Come on. Really? What do parents do to show favouritism? Are you treating one adult child so differently that their siblings are complaining? Just another question to ponder.

Our adult children are just that, adults. Perhaps they will take notice that a father goes to a sporting event with the AK that appreciates a good sport match. Maybe a mother takes her daughter who lives closest to her on the most outings for dinners. And as parents, we notice that some AKs will have different opportunities to be with us, to holiday with us, have regular visits, and get our personal time. There will be a balancing act that needs to be noticed and maybe even discussed. Does favouritism enter into these actions? I can only speak for myself, but I am not convinced I could pick a favourite child on any day. How can parents see the AK who lives miles away as much as the one who lives down the street? Can parents financially assist the AK who has lost their job while the other is gainfully employed? These are a few of the dilemmas we may face.

Sibling rivalry is real because we do treat each adult child in a special way. We are different parents to each child, as we raised them at different times and with different perspectives. We need to be open and honest about that, without making excuses, without talking behind backs or excluding a sibling. Serious business. And we thought sibling rivalry was only for children. Ha.

10.

Can We Be Friends?

Years ago, when my kids were little, I created a story that I didn't want to be friends with my own children. My values included respect for and from my children. I valued the love of a child and loving a being who needed me. They were our children, and we were their parents. A relationship with boundaries. My husband and I thought we understood that relationship of being parents versus friends. I read books and went to lectures given by specialists in parenting. We worked to be Backbone parents, the kind that Barbara Colorosso, a parenting expert in the 90's recommended. Not Brickwalls, too strict, or Jellyfishes, too loosey goosey. Somehow the version of Backbone parent fit us nicely. Or so we thought. Our definition of family was not that we were all friends with equal rights.

When my friends told me how they loved being "friends" with their teenage daughters, I could feel myself passing judgement. Surely they could see my eye roll. What? How can you parent a child, deliver lessons, and deliver natural and logical consequences to a "friend?" I just didn't get it! And there were many topics I discussed with my friends that I did not feel my children needed to hear. My kids were not my friends.

Today, as I experience life with adult children, I have changed my mind. I like being their friend. I treasure our moments of exchanging ideas, chatting about recipes, planning an outing with them, hearing about their day. Working alongside them on a project is one of my happy places. My heart is full when we are being friendly. This transition is one that was slow and bumpy. With one AK, I am still to find the right balance.

Mom Mode

No one is happier than a mom whose grown kid has called to say hi. Nothing else. Just hi.

-"Moms of Bigs" Insta post

When my adult kids speak and I am in a "mom" mode, I offer suggestions, seek solutions, and make corrections. With my friends, I ponder more. I ask questions. I listen. Can I become like a friendly neighbour, a friend, with my AKs? Of course that is possible. With a solid, intentional effort. And I do appreciate the gentle nudging from my husband, "Gill, they are 30 years old. Let them make their own decisions." Thank you.

Sometime in 2000, my youngest gave me a call on a landline. He was at high school, so I can pinpoint the year. I was still very much in "mom" mode. My reactions were so not that of a trusting friend.

"Hi, Mom," I heard my youngest child. "I forgot my lunch."

"Oh geez," I responded. "Do you have money to buy something at the cafeteria? When is your next class? Can you get home and back before that? Could I pick up something and drive it over for you?"

I'm not sure I took a breath. Just one question after another. One solution or suggestion piled on the last. That's me. A solution seeker, problem solver, brainstorming queen, fixer.

"Mom, mom, WAIT!" I heard a breath of silence on the other end of the line. "I just wanted you to put my lunch bag in the fridge for tomorrow. It's sitting at the back door. My friend is sharing her lunch with me." Truly, I was disappointed. The rescue was not needed. But it brought me to a pause, a ponder perhaps. Why did I need to solve this issue? Didn't I think my son could manage a missed lunch? Really?

"WAIT" is written on a small sign I have perched at eye level on a shelf in my coaching office. In sessions with a life coach, the client is to do the talking. This four-letter reminder is one we, the problem solving moms, might wish to tattoo on our wrists. Or dangle from the peak of a baseball cap, constantly in view. W…A…I…T…simply reminds me to ask myself, **"Why Am I Talking?"**

As a mother of younger children, I felt programmed to find answers to questions, to take an action to relieve someone else of a potential problem. I was the rescuer, the saviour, a protector of sorts. I needed to create a problem-solving list, offer advice. That's what we were programmed to do as parents. At least that's what I thought then. This mode of being is what has to change if I am to develop a solid relationship with my adult children. I cannot be the "fixer." Friends don't fix. They listen.

In fact, our children absolutely do not want us to come up with suggestions, alternatives, answers. At this stage in our relationship, any suggestion comes across as criticism, a sign that we don't have faith in them and that they don't have the resources to solve their own issues. Of course, this is not our intent, but this is how we are received.

Play

I am taking the opportunity to give this "friend" thing a good college try. At times I recognize I am backsliding into the dreaded *parenting* world, and I have to remind myself: friendly neighbour, no attachments, no ego involved. Just be a friend. Ponder, ask, listen.

The best times are the treasured moments when we are being friendly to one another. When we are interacting in a relaxed dance of conversation. Laughing at the same jokes, engaged in an activity of fun or adventure. Or just sharing a meal with free flowing conversation.

At our cottage card table, we often giggle about the adult conversations, the swearing, the sexual references, and the rudeness we share with our grown kids. Our large family loves playing cards. *May I?* and *Screw Your Neighbour* are the two favourite games of choice. Even when we say those game names, I am reminded we have set ourselves up for adult/friend time.

Our eldest niece 'Molly' set the pace of our parent/adult kid mood at these card games. Years ago, when she was in her early twenties, someone (okay, maybe it was me) offered up a sexual favour (to my husband) for a much-needed card. "Hello??" came a voice from the far end of the table, "I'm sitting right here!" It was Molly. The whole table laughed. F.Y.I. My husband did not give me the card.

Later in the game, after a vigorous round of play, a slew of creative swear words erupted from my brother-in-law. And we heard a delicate, "I'm still here," from Molly. Somehow she could time that in the seconds of quiet. This little chant of "I'm still here" has become a saying for the adult kids around the table. They love the moment when they can tease us with their supposed innocence and embarrassment.

This is a moment of friendship for me. When we acknowledge our differences and joke about expected behaviours, our separateness in age, and just giggle. No judgement. A nice little reminder that it can be a free for all in a multi-generational cut-throat card game.

The Transition

My good friend, Bob, tells me, "You know I want to be friends with my kids, Gill." And yes, I do know. His girls are adults, living with partners, one about to be married. He is a wonderful dad who would and does do a lot for his girls. Their relationship seemed to morph without too much effort from Dad and little girl to Dad with adult daughters. His wife agrees. "Bob has never had to be the disciplinarian. I did that. They have always run to him for support." I wonder, do dads have an easier time growing into the parents of grown daughters? Are dads usually more "friendly?"

His wife says, "No, he doesn't have an easier time; his relationship just stayed the same. So now when the girls come to him for help and comfort and support, the problems and asks aren't as little anymore. They want big stuff. Big asks. And it is hard for him to say no. Guess we have to pick our battles."

Turning into a friend to my adult children has not been a quick transition. But I think we are there now. We holiday with them like we vacation with friends. Some bills are picked up by us, but the adult kids proudly pick up the tab or cook a meal, buy cool gifts, and offer up fun entertainment for us all. We learn new drinking games from them and just watch them, of course. And they patiently learn card games from us. We ski together and golf together and generally have a relaxing time when we converse. Our life and decisions are not tied to theirs, but we involve them. And we converse before major changes are made.

The whole being a friend thing has opened up a more relaxed relationship. I am more respectful of them. And I feel more confident asking, "Do you want some advice? Some comfort? Or just an open ear?" What a difference that has made. Have you heard of this perspective before? How do you set boundaries around your relationships with your adult kids? How do you open doors to make the relationship stronger? It is worth exploring. Maybe a glass of wine and a chat with your own Sisterhood of Mothers will spark ideas and answers.

> *It brings me great joy to be friends with my parents and aunts and uncles, and it really is a relationship like no other–sometimes friends, sometimes guides, sometimes other things that I can't articulate…*
>
> -'Molly', after reading the Chapter

11.

Holidays and Other Get-togethers

Hanging out with your grown-up kids is like visiting the best parts of your life.

-Insta post July 2022

I couldn't agree more. Hanging with my AKs is so fun! Their love of board games, skiing, golfing, and hosting great parties just reminds me that their lives are reflecting the best parts of us. Maybe it is the sharing of common values that brings us family joy. But the work to get to that " hanging out" place? Ugh. It's like herding cats. "Oh, I can't be there THAT weekend!" "Can't we do something else?" Or my favourite, "Are you and Dad paying? 'Coz we can't afford that."

We all want to be together as a family. Or at least they say they want to be together. But when each child has a life and a partner or spouse, the planning can be serious work. Email after email or Facetime after Facetime or text after text. And the family chat? OMG. That just gets crazy! Yes. We love spending time together. We thrive on our travel adventures. We can't wait until the next family trip. But will that be in December? Or February? Or March? That's the challenge with adult kids. They are busy. They have their own lives. Remember when you could just put them in a carry basket, plunk them in the car, and go when and where you wished? Recall the days when your summer holidays meant you packed the clothes and they just wore them. Or not. Remember? Ya. Not that easy anymore. Our children were raised to be independent and self-sufficient. That was really one of my primary intentions as a parent. I value independence and the ability to make my own decisions and choices. I wanted that for my children.

And now, all that independence just gets in the way of us being together! Jobs and significant others and the families of significant others and budgeting issues all get in the way of planning time together. Christmas or other holidays must be planned months, if not years in advance. And yes, I understand it is harder when all three of your kids, like mine, live in three different countries, in three different time zones.

Balancing Responsibilities

My girlfriends go to concerts with their adult daughters. They travel south as families, all the adult children, significant others, and grandbabies. Do they like their arrangement? One Dad told me, "It's nice to have the whole family together. But I do like to see them go and leave us for two weeks on our own." Now this family lives very close to one another all the time. If you are far from your kids, like we are, those visits may become more precious. I am new to this, so I can't say. But other parents visit their adult children's homes several times a year. Howard and Ellie have a "granny suite" in the downstairs of their son's home on the west coast. Lois and John have a regular Airbnb they rent, just down the street from their son's home. They visit for holidays during the winter, spring, and fall. The kids come east to the cottage for summer breaks.

What are the comments about these visits to their AKs' homes? "They (adult children) are busy. Everyone is on the go. And we join them. We don't get much say in what we do. We follow along with whatever plans the kids have made." Both say pretty much the same thing. And the summer get-togethers? Flipped switch. "We are always busy making meals, cleaning up afterwards, and the kids take the boats and enjoy hanging at the cottage. They don't really take on much work. Just like when they were teenagers." Hmm I wonder. We created that beast, didn't we?

In another family I know, the adult children pull their own weight. Always have. "My boys love to barbecue and cook dinners. Then when they work around the place, I fix them a nice meal. They are so appreciative of what they have. And they still do the manual work to keep up the property." My neighbour has a beehive of activity around her home regularly. Her adult kids assist her regularly with season changes of garden planting, Christmas tree lighting, and even snow removal. They gather for Sunday dinners and holiday celebrations.

Those parents worked hard to instill a work ethic in their children before they reached adulthood. Everyone pitches in. The work is divided, and that is the fun! Seems the groundwork was laid in the teen years and continued. Amazing what can happen when the boundaries are set and defined. So cool to learn that, even at this late stage.

Official Holidays

One night I overheard my two friends chatting about Christmas holiday plans. You can insert any holiday time you wish. Each woman has four adult children, in-laws, partners of AKs, and grandchildren. There is a lot of input around what to do for Christmas, a holiday meant for time shared, giving and receiving of gifts, and celebrating our love for each other. Many non-Christians take the opportunity to celebrate at this time of year, so this is not solely a religious holiday.

The activities that come around this 25th date, or other holiday dates, may have significant meaning to families. Holiday traditions are precious, so meaningful to us that we may forget the needs of others. How do we pause and take the time to embrace the wishes of all our family members? I know there are some unique ways to celebrate, and I have seen lots of families embrace rituals created to suit the family as it has evolved to be.

There are parents who don't get to visit often with their family units. And parents who have divorced or separated and have to share their AK time with ex-spouses. And then there are the in-laws of our AKs, who also want to spend time with your adult child, as their child's partner. We have a lot of sharing going on. And that has the potential to bring anxiety and stress. Our AKs will feel the push and pull. They get to share the stress. Not a good share. I try my best to accommodate the needs of others, without being too demanding and pushing too much. The way I make my request can be taken as an invitation or inflict guilt. Have you heard yourself make those guilt-inspiring requests? "Didn't you stay with your in-laws last Christmas?"

"Don't you have time to spend one day here?" These questions seem simple enough, yet they are guilt creators, stress builders. When my friends and I chat with one another, we recognize the error in our ways.

Articles and tales of holiday stress are endless. Families who have members who fight at the sight of each other, still feel a need to gather. What's with that? Families who do not have money to manage day to day living feel compelled to buy gifts. Expensive ones. Holidays can be seriously nerve wracking. And yet, we somehow still have expectations of our AKs. Sometimes we forget to balance our traditions with our true intentions.

The conversation I overheard with the two mothers of four was a bit of a list. Their eldest adult child, and the second one, and the third, and the last. And each of their plans. One AK in each family had no idea what their spouse's family had planned, so was unable to commit to anything. Right then. "Could everyone please wait until we find out?" was their request. So, everyone else in the family just sat and waited on the one couple. Can we see how one little request to plan might add one big stress? Family life can be a time of compromise and creativity.

Christmas "Time"

One of my very clever cottage friends has a Christmas "time," five days set aside for celebratory gatherings. She invites each child to visit as it suits them, and she is prepared each day for some kind of time with them. Even her guest room is fluffed and prepped. There is no turkey dinner and all that could entail, just comfort food, easy and wholesome. A time to sit around the table and enjoy some banter. Some wine. For her it works. For her family it works. "Last year two of the kids coordinated with one another to come together for two nights. They did the work to coordinate. And they even made sure their brother didn't mind."

Some families have the "year on, year off" system in place. We tried that. The "year off" sure was initially depressing. Even the two single adult kids did not come home. I remember sulking and telling my husband, "We will never again spend holidays alone at home." I hope I didn't guilt my kids and tell them how lonely we were. That's a thing, you know. Moms adding to their adult children's feeling of guilt.

And then, after all our feeling sorry for ourselves, the magic of Christmas came true. Another good family friend invited us over to enjoy Christmas dinner with all her adult children. What fun we had! Our spirits lifted the minute we walked in the back door and heard the banter between siblings and their partners. Nothing beats a good kitchen gathering.

New Traditions

Our AKs are busy. Those with tiny tots want to start their own family traditions. Those who are single may not have the finances to come home, buy gifts, or take time off work. I am not sure why it has taken me so long to realise our adult kids don't need my, our, added pressures. Some parents have figured this out much earlier than me. I guess I didn't listen. So, today, I pledge to relax. Hold me accountable. Reducing guilt for our children equates to fewer expectations from us. Don't we want to be with them more than we want to have it our way? Maybe there is a way to take all of their needs into the decisions we make for all of us.

Our wine chats are so full of new and interesting ways to live life with extended families and share our times in different ways. I learn so much when I listen with an open heart and a willingness to let go of my control. Maybe restrictions set by a need for tradition no longer fit. Maybe there is a way to respect the time we have together and craft it the way that suits us all.

Our past Christmas together we had one day where we actually ranked the three available activities: skating, hiking, and skiing. We voted. Skating won. And even those who didn't vote for skating had the most wonderful day. To get to skating we had to hike. And the temperatures were so low, the movement in skating kept us all warm. Yup. With a little give and take, we created the best of days for everyone! Our family time is worth all the hassle of planning. And some traditions may have to be sacrificed…for the long game.

12.

Maybe Baby

"Geez, I raised YOU! You turned out okay,"

said a wise woman, NEVER.

This argument that you raised your child, so you know it all, does not hold any water when your child has a child of their own. All the thinking about babies is modernized. Some of the things we did with our babies would not pass today's "responsible parent" test. For example, bumper pads for cribs. We had them. Our kids survived. Today, the rule is no bumper pads. Remember this when you start to think about how you handled your baby, and want to pass the knowledge along. Today, baby raising is just not the same. Even my family doctor husband reminds me, "Don't be telling a new mom what to do. There is so much new science." How are we to be as parents to parents, and grandparents to their babies?

We are not blessed to be grandparents…yet. We hope to be. I hear it is the most wonderful time of life. Pure fun and at the end of the day, you hand the baby back to their parents and get a full night's sleep. All the bonuses and none of the worries. I can hardly wait. And then, the real stories are told.

When the wine flows. Annie tells us, "My son says his wife does not want to dress their child in gender specific colours." Barb leads the way,"Males wear pink all the time now. It's quite fashionable." "What's gender neutral?" asks someone. Greys and purples, maybe a green, we ponder. "Who gets to decide?" I ask.

One friend told me, "My grandchild doesn't get a soother until she reaches six months. Pacifiers cause 'nipple confusion'. Google that!" she added. Her daughter's midwife told her, "Just soothe with other methods." I wondered if that midwife had any kids of her own.

Birthing New Methods

Midwives and home births. WTF? My first introduction to a home birth was frightening for me. I could not imagine a blow-up pool filled with water for the delivery, in the living room. I remember how we "fought" to get our husbands in the room beside us. At this home birth, the husband was there, but the doula and midwife directed the mom's breathing. The mom ended up rushed to the emergency room and had to be given blood. Dad was literally left holding the baby while mom went away in an ambulance. Exactly what trauma did our birthing rooms in the hospital cause? These are the thoughts left for the friends at our wine time.

My wine sipping friends and I wonder: "I am not sure why home births are making such a comeback. I thought modern medicine was safer." "Maybe there is quiet for the first baby, but what the heck do you do with a two-year-old at the birth of a second?" "They don't watch. Or do they?" So many questions. Thank goodness I don't have to deal with this. And thanks also that I have time to perfect my "no judgement" here look. "Oh, that's nice. A home birth. How lovely." Smile. Nod. 'No judgement' look. Good luck to me.

When my own mother was a child in Scotland she remembers hearing neighbours calling for her mom, my grandmother. "Come quick Maggie, it's me Mam's time." A new baby was about to be delivered. There was no doctor present. Just my Grandma Maggie. And babies died. Mothers died. And the healthcare system "evolved." But not today. The spectrum of thinking about happy, safe births once again includes the option of home birth and everything in between.

Pregnancy and childbirth and infants are totally different in today's world. It seems every ten years they decide to change up the sleeping position of the infant: sideways, front sleeping, now fully back sleeping, without blankets. The babies of today have some cute little sleeping sacks, with arm holes. But remember, none of those crib bumpers. They kill.

I understand these decisions are not to be taken lightly by mom and dad. Secretly, we know babies are resilient. But for the love of God, your own life, and the relationship you have with the childbearing adult children, do NOT offer up any suggestions. Find those zipped lips! Bite your tongue. Any suggestions will be taken as criticism. No one likes to be criticised. Take your pointer finger, glue it to your thumb, and follow your lip line. Zip it. Then smile to the new mom, "You've got this." Or send a thumbs up emoji. Oh, this generation of parents are serious.

In my "research" and in our conversations about how to offer up suggestions, I have discovered that most, if not all, unsolicited advice is considered criticism. If someone has not directly requested your advice, your ideas, your way of doing things, do not offer.

The simplest of techniques, we decided in one wine-filled chat, is to ask, "Might I offer a suggestion?" or "Are you open to hear my advice?" And wait. You have to wait to get permission. One friend offered up this more subtle introduction: "In my experience, this is what I have seen." And then offer your observations. Again, we have to be open to hearing how that suggestion landed. "What did you think about that?" "Would you consider that?" We parents of adults have to practice and make some mistakes along the way. We each have to find what rolls off our tongue with some comfort. And find what works with your own adult child. They are all different.

As sarcastic as I can be, I know that an open mind goes a long way. I know we have to respect that our adult children have done some thinking, often with their partners, and made some decisions. Educated decisions perhaps. From a well-subscribed podcast host, blogger, or Instagrammer. Researched decisions, maybe. Just like us, our adult kids get to make their own mistakes. That's what pains us so much.

Their Rules Now

One friend has family members who have been 'barred' from seeing their granddaughter until they learn to use the pronouns "they" and "them." You know. No he or she or her or him. Non-binary pronouns. These grandparents have to learn more than just the "no judgement" look. Now they have to change their way of thinking and speaking, too. This is really hard for our generation that has lived long lives looking at a baby in pink and cooing, "Isn't she pretty." No longer allowed. Stop it! We have to make serious efforts to respect the wishes of our adult children, even though we may not fully understand them. Especially if we want to have our grandchildren in our lives. The place to voice the confusion is when you are pouring the wine with friends. Not arguing with your grandchild's parents.

Do you think the decision to raise a non-binary child was made before or after the gender reveal party? You know the balloon popping, cake exploding photos posted and spread on social media. "Oh look! The sparkles are blue. They are having a male!" But better not call him "him," or "he," give him blue booties or a little bow tie. Too complicated. And how are we to know which way our own adult children or their other "baby-parent" will side on these gender issues? I am baffled. And a tad sarcastic.

One young couple, Drew and Kristen, even forewarned their grandparents-to-be that the baby's name was to be a gender-neutral name. "Practise your game face so you don't overreact when you first hear it," was our advice to our friend. And our friend, Grandma, did practise regularly. We tested her. Lots! Haven, Ellis, Morgan, Kennedy, Indiana, Jasper. "Bert" someone offers up, "for a girl," they add. Nope. None of us could hold our game face. Unacceptable, we all agreed. And we even know a "Bert," Roberta.

The baby with the gender-neutral name had cousins named Rose and Lily. Clearly these adult mom-sisters didn't even think alike. One daughter has Rose and Lily, the other daughter has a pretty little daughter named Jones. Come on. Let's get serious here. How are we as parents/grandparents supposed to know what to expect? Am I even allowed to call the baby Jones pretty?

Where Do Babies Come From?

We are stumped. There are all kinds of permutations, options, and choices with childbearing. Invitro fertilisation, surrogate parents, siblings who become surrogate parents, those in same-sex relationships who want to have children, combining both invitro and a surrogate. And there are AKs who choose childlessness. And there are single women who choose to parent on their own. And single men who make the choice also. And in the end, babies are babies. And all babies need a village. A loving, supportive village. Can we be that? As parents and grandparents, can we willingly support our own AK's choices for their own families? These are the tough questions that might be raised as we reach this stage in our AK's lives. How do we prepare ourselves? What can we do now to make ourselves open to a way of parenting that might be unfamiliar? Guess we are back to the "know yourself" suggestion. And maybe the "stay open" advice. Do I need these signs in my office, too?

Our lives will change when and if we become grandparents. All the joys will be there. All our hearts will be filled and warmed. And we will have to watch ourselves as we interact with our adult children as the parents of our grandchildren. We, as grandparents, are there for the love of everyone. The love, not the opinions, and the judgements, and the lectures. Ah... sometimes so difficult.

PART 4

Who Am I?

13.

Dangerous Expectations…

Most of my wine sipping friends are close to my age, or at least over 50 years young. Women who had children at 25 to 35 ish years of age. Our adult children are no longer our sole focus. The daily concerns we have might be more closely governed by our own ageing parents, our own health, our own retirement plans. We have been called the "sandwich" generation. Those pulled between expectations from both ageing parents and adult children.

Although our adult children play a less important role in directing our day, we do still have expectations that they will be around, in some way. Some moms wish the adult kids were in their lives more. Some moms wish their AKs would get a job and get out of the house! But still visit. Everyone seeks to find their own comfort zone. Through communication and boundary setting we can find the balance that suits both us and our adult children. And remember, research shows we are more concerned about these relationships, and have higher expectations than our adult kids.

My husband and I have cared for and supported and loved each of our children for a long time. We supported them physically, financially, and emotionally. Of course we have a stake in the game. Understandable. But does that mean we have big expectations? Should we have any expectations at all? Hmm. I feel this could be dangerous. Expectations are typically red flags that someone might be disappointed.

For now, we can be sure that parents care more about this difficult, tumultuous, wild ride with our adult kids than they do. We need to be and behave in a way that allows the relationships to bloom.

The Devil's In The Details

So what do you expect of them? And, yes, what are they asking of you? What do they expect from you? Seems simple enough to learn, if everyone speaks respectfully to one another. And if both parties even know what they want. Expectations are tricky to recognize. Usually, we have insight into our expectations after they do not get met. We might want to think more about our true, perhaps hidden expectations because they play a huge role in our relationships with our adult kids.

Sometimes the expectations of one another just naturally, organically develop. Many of us have ideas about what we expect from adults, whether they are our children or not. Our AKs are adults. But, do we have different expectations for them as our sweat and blood off-spring? Do they have different expectations of us, as parents? We need to know more than if they want to be friends or friendly.

Figuring out the nuances of your relationship with your big kid is no simple task.
They need to talk.
They need to be alone.
They need a hug.
They need some space.
They need you to stick up for them.
They need you to stay out of it. They need you to stand firm.
They need you to be flexible.
It's exhausting.
The best and most important thing for you to be is kind to yourself.
You will need it.

-MOMS OF BIGS estherjoygoetz.com

"Why don't they want our advice?" my doctor friend Dave asked me. His own son, Connor, also a family physician, came to work at his medical practice. Connor had been working in a similar medical practice for two years. After he broke up with his last girlfriend, and divided the household goods, Connor came back to his hometown. He didn't move back to the family home; he just went to work in his parents' medical office. And now Connor can't decide whether to stay and work their office or move to another location. Dave obviously has some ideas about what to consider when making such a decision, after all they share the same profession. But Connor doesn't want his advice. So they just don't talk about it. Dave's retirement or restructuring plan is on hold.

This is a frustration for parents. Our adult kids may not wish to hear what we have to say. And on some days I can say to myself, well why should they? What exactly do we know about their world? And on other days, I think, wait…I have valuable experiences to share. I am an intelligent being and my AKs should benefit from my advice. I expected that they would. But nope. They do not.

Just like my designer friend Jo. She has years of experience decorating homes. Her places always look spectacular. It would make sense to me that her adult kids make use of these talents. "Hannah has moved into her new condo", my friend Jo tells me. Hannah is Jo's 28- year-old daughter.

"Cool," I responded. "How's she liking it?"

Jo continues, "You know how you make suggestions to kids and they don't seem to take them? Then later they realise you were right?" "Yep. Happens all the time." Again, me being sarcastic.

"Well, Hannah just went out and bought a new ceiling fan for her upstairs spare room. Her boyfriend installed it last night. I suggested she get one on Day 1. Before the condo was even built. She could have had a fan when she moved in."

"Frustrating, isn't it?" I side with my friend Jo. "You could have saved her time and money." Jo gives a perfunctory eye roll.

"You didn't say 'I told you so' did you?" Jo shakes her head. Clever woman. Knows when to stick out her tongue and bite down. Remember that podcast, Bite Your Tongue? It is named that for a good reason.

Chances are Hannah didn't declare, "Mom, you were right!" If you ever, ever, hear those words, hug that child as tightly as a big mama bear. Soak in the moment. And hug them some more.

This is one of the stories we parents know to be true. Often our adult kids deem our experiences useless. Our advice falls on deaf ears. It doesn't matter that Jo is an experienced designer. Doesn't matter that Dave is a fellow physician. Jo is Hannah's mom. Dave is Connor's dad. That's who was talking when the adult kids weren't listening, their parent. A mom and/or dad doesn't always get much of an ear. Unless they are asked.

Accountable To Whom?

According to Dr. Larry Nelson of SSEA, our experiences are nothing like what the current "emerging adults" are living. He actually suggests we throw out all we learned when we were young adults. Our advice, based on our past experiences, is not relevant. And most AKs do not want to hear "in my day…" or "this is what I did…" Our adult children are getting lots of information from their own research. Answers to questions and problems are easy to find quickly. This culture of adult children use social media for all their learning. Our son renovated a full house using what he learned on Google. And yes, a little help from his Dad, but mainly Youtube videos. Their exercise programs can be online, their course work is often off-campus and online, their medical advice and records can be found there, banking, booking vacations, investments, flights, accommodations…you get the culture. Their every question, desire, and need can be satisfied with a simple key tap on their computer or phone. Parents are not a resource. You can google that, too!

So if our adult children do not want advice, what do they expect of us? How do we need to be for them? I am pretty sure my Sisterhood of Moms have told me our adult children want empathy, not answers. They want us to listen, hear and understand. Ask questions, stay curious. That is a repeated message. Seems that what is really meant by "zip it" and "bite your tongue" is really don't talk, just listen. Again, not my strong suit, but I am trying. I am reminded often that unsolicited advice is received as criticism. This quiet is part of respecting my adult children. Being a friendly neighbour, perhaps. Accepting that they are adults… mostly.

Defining Expectations

The thing about expectations is that if they are not met, we are sadly disappointed. And if we do have them? We had better find out what they are. Sometimes, we don't even know what we expect until we feel disappointed. And that is bad timing. Remember, our AKs have expectations, too. Of us, and themselves. Do our AKs expect money? Do they expect us to babysit? Do they express their needs as expectations or requests?

Sometimes we create our own heartbreaks through expectation.
                        -Ryan Reynolds

Expectations can create family issues. If our adult kids don't ask us to visit, we might assume they prefer we don't. If we would like our adult children to come help paint the cottage they use, how will they know if we don't communicate that? Guess we are back to communication and boundary setting and being true to ourselves, our values, our principles. And yes, we all will want to gain insight into our unspoken expectations. We and our adult kids will want to engage in that thinking!

My 33-year-old daughter, who lives an ocean away, sent me

a cartoon. The caption read: How I saw myself at 30 / How I am at 30. On the left was a picture of a woman holding a baby. On the right, the same woman lovingly caressing a dog! Very cute. Very funny. Very true. Charlie, my daughter's adopted dog, is her foundation and when she crosses the ocean to visit us, she misses Charlie the most. This dog makes her house a home. Charlie even has a dog "nanny" because my daughter works and travels a lot. And right now, Charlie has a foster dog living with him. I guess the comic she sent me suggests this is not how she expected to be living. But we are all good with this, until she calls me Charlie's "Grandma." I draw the line there.

Most of the time, our expectations are left unspoken. They kind of hover around us, within us, and sometimes in our subconscious mind. We can have no idea of our "expectations" until a situation occurs. I had no idea I would not like the "Dog Grandma" title until it was put out there. Our expectations are so tied to our beliefs and our values, our own personal understandings of life. Trust me on this, lots of times we have no idea what our beliefs or values or expectations are until we face an event that just doesn't sit well with us.

Why does it bother me to be called a dog's "Grandma?" Some people could just laugh at that. Some fully embrace and encourage. But it triggers something in me. My inside voices are hints to me about what might be going on. "I am not a grandma at all. I don't want a dog to replace a grandchild. I want a grandchild. My daughter is replacing her need for a real child with this dog. She will never have a child if she allows all her love to go into this animal. My daughter will never know the love of a child if she continues to pour all her time and affection into this animal…" Yup. This is what goes on in my head. These thoughts are not real. They are simply thoughts. Truth or non-truth cannot even be argued.

Have you ever heard your brain go on one of these side trips? We can really drive ourselves into stress, anxiety, and depression with thoughts. Unfounded, unsubstantiated, illogical thoughts. This journey of examining ourselves, our thoughts, our beliefs, our expectations is exhausting.

The Unexamined Life...

Our expectations of our children can be very dangerous. Children can sense when parents are unhappy with them or ashamed of them or embarrassed. But they can also feel shame, embarrassment, or guilt because of their own insecurities. I cannot even begin to explain how dangerous shame and guilt can be for us or for our AKs. Brené Brown has done the research. Watch her Ted Talks! What is relevant is that we come to understand the dangers of expectations when they are left unspoken or unexamined.

This chapter offers directions to do a little heavy work. Become introspective. I urge myself, you, and our children to ask each other what we expect of one another. We know we have expectations of our AKs. I sure do. When they don't meet those expectations, we might blame them. Our minds may ruminate. Ugh. I bet as your friends discuss this book, you will hear many examples of us, the parents of AKs, being annoyed because our expectations have not been met. It starts with: they don't clean up after themselves, their rooms are a mess, their homework isn't done. And then the responsibilities get bigger and the demands get more pressing. Now it's: they quit a job and don't have another to go to, they went on an expensive holiday and now can't make the mortgage payment, they married the totally wrong person and are in a vicious divorce. The list can go on and on.

Unspoken expectations can create family issues. When we don't examine and speak our intentions, our expectations, others will assume and create their own versions. Guess we are back to open communication, boundary setting and being true to ourselves, our values, and our principles. And yes, we will want to gain insight into our unspoken expectations. We and our adult kids will want to engage in that self-exploration for awareness.

14.

Values, Foundation, Grounding

Take a deep breath. The biggest you have taken all day... Release your breath. And find your foundation.
-Words from my wise yoga instructor. Sometimes we need the reminder.

My yoga practice grounds me. I set an intention to get to my mat for at least 30 minutes each day. The Peloton can sit vacant for days at a time, but my mat is changed and washed regularly. I sweat there. My online yoga instructor is a warm, insightful woman who reminds me to slow down, move intentionally, and breathe deeply. The reminders to "find your roots," "return to your foundation," and "ground yourself" are words I repeat to myself on and off the mat. My coaching clients hear these terms often.

As a parent, I try to remember to return to my own foundational values each time I chat with our adult kids. I find this makes listening and interacting easier. Thank goodness I see yoga as a practice. Never really at perfection, always in the state of learning and trying over and over again. We can forgive ourselves when we admit we are still in the learning process.

What Are Your Values?

Small deliberate tweaks infused with your values can make a huge difference in your life.

-Susan David, *Emotional Agility*

Have you done any work with finding your values? My simplest coaching for value activities involves listing your pet peeves, taking note of what really pushes your buttons and getting to the root of your feelings. Seeing what riles you up helps bring insight into what is important to you. Values are not constant, although most of us tend to hang in the same realm of what is important to us, our "principles" of living. Our values will get set and reset, examined and questioned and rediscovered, sometimes when we least expect it.

Picture me sitting on my front porch. I am having a nice day and life seems to be going really well. Then suddenly, some a-hole goes speeding through the stop sign at the end of my street. I wish for a "go-go gadget" arm to stretch out and grab them right back to come to a full stop. When people act without regard for others, judgmental me labels them inconsiderate and self-centred. Yup, one of my pet peeves. Acting with zero concern for anyone else's safety or well-being. I am instantly annoyed at such behaviour, which is rooted in my own value to have respect for others. To me this is basic stuff: be considerate and mindful of those around us.

Another way to discover your values is to remember what really warms your heart. An act of love for me is having my morning coffee mug on the counter beside a freshly brewed pot of coffee. I know I am loved when I wake to that. My eldest is the best at coffee making and even frothing the milk. Now my youngest has caught on and he steps up. Their father has been doing that for years. It's what keeps us basking in the little moments of love. I value being remembered and considered. It's even sweeter when I don't have to ask.

Clashing Values

Our family has a way of knowing our values and occasionally, someone, okay, maybe me, will forget if they are distracted or self- absorbed. When that happens, there may be a burst of anger, disappointment, or annoyance. That's when we practice taking a breath and returning to our foundation, remembering what is important, and not getting stuck within the "button pushing" moment. Like when we are planning holiday time. Remembering our intentions, what is at the foundation of our wishes, will keep us focused in a mindful manner.

"She is so selfish," my friend Annie complained about her 34-year- old daughter-in-law. "I think she loves their dog more than my son." Annie paused as she heard herself. "Let me just say she treats the dog very well."

Annie's story is one of frustration around not seeing her son as much as she would like. She is not alone. Lots of parents miss their adult children. Perhaps this reflects one of their values around family. Annie's son, Jack, and daughter-in-law, Sophie, had planned to join the family vacation at a rented ski chalet. The rented chalet didn't allow dogs. Sophie and Jack had just bought a new puppy. One of them had to stay home with the pup, and it was apparent that it would be Sophie. Jack would be visiting alone for a shorter period of time. Annie was miffed. The planning required to get all three adult kids and their partners in one place at the same time was not an easy task. With this new puppy, Annie would not see her daughter-in-law and would have only three days with Jack, instead of seven, because of a dog. How our AKs love their animals!

Clearly Annie values time with her family. And some family members value training time for their new puppy. Simple, when put on paper. But to a mom who wants as much time as she can get with her son, not quite good enough. Having to choose between a dog and family time was an easy choice for Annie. Her adult kids had other values in play for their decision making at that time.

(BTW...this dog was bought after the rental had been made. Annie is not that insensitive. I am sure he was a "rescue dog," which I always thought meant the dog was good at saving people. Apparently not. I hear my AKs' eye rolls from here.)

Annie later realized, after a little porch chat involving a glass of pinot, that she respected her family's decision making based on their own values. They were taking responsibility for their own decisions. After a deep breath and finding her foundation, she felt comforted knowing they would still have "family time." The group might be smaller, the time frame might be shorter, but her family would all arrive and have time to visit. Not like she expected. No, it wasn't. Is it worth arguing about? Should she complain the whole time that she only had a three-day visit? Remind her son that Sophie preferred the company of the dog? You can fill in the other rants, and we all know the answer. NO. Of course not.

We get into these traps. And hence need the reminder to breathe. Find our foundation. Practice. And go easy on ourselves and our kids when we forget. We are still learning.

Breaking Habits

Clients have shared that they sometimes value peace and quiet; therefore, they give into a demand from their AK so the conversation will end without argument. That pattern probably started earlier in the relationship, perhaps when the AKs were teens. The pleas from teens of "MOM, all my friends stay out until 2 a.m. Midnight curfews suck. Come on, MOM. Be real." And on and on it goes, until Mom hears herself saying "Okay, 2 a.m. but no later." All to avoid further arguments and discussion. This pattern is tough to break. Easier if it was never started. But thankfully, the pattern can be broken.

Parents of adult children who have returned home have shared how tough it is to break old habits of their own and the AKs'. Maybe the AKs still don't do their own laundry or clean the kitchen, pay rent or offer to cook meals. Their actions do not speak to respect for their parents. They may not speak to the consideration of others in the house. And moms still back down on their personal requests and wishes because moms don't want to rock the boat. Many a mom has been known to say, "Oh, it's just easier if I do it myself." Really? Some have worse complaints than laundry and kitchen cleaning. Not every behaviour can be ignored.

We can get caught in this kind of situation and end up doing all the work. It took me a long time and lots of prodding by my husband to show the kids how to do something the first time, do a bit of teaching and demonstrating, and then leave it to them. And then stick to our guns when the deed wasn't complete. These patterns can slip so early, and when we are faced with adult kids, the work will be harder. Yet the rewards will be lifelong. "Think of the long game" is a useful strategy in these circumstances. Making one moment easier can cause many moments of turmoil and struggle.

One of the Facebook groups I belong to had a unique response from a professional house organizer about adult children who had moved home and continued their adolescent behaviours around cleaning a kitchen. She advised going through the kitchen and organizing a clearly designated spot for everything. And she meant everything. If you could complete this task with your adult kids, all the better. Set rules around "Everything has a place and everything in its place." Then there is no argument. Nothing personal. Either the dish did or did not go back into its proper spot. Clean cut. State the expectation and agree to have it met by all. Save the questioning and ambiguity. Save the argument. Kind of like setting boundaries. Boundaries that fit the situation, not necessary the people. Boundaries are guidelines. They offer up methods, skills, tools to stay in clear communication and be true to our values. Boundaries create guidelines that work for the long game.

Julie, a single mom of a 25-year-old, told me, "My son hasn't left the basement all week. He quit his job. I have no idea what he does down there, except the television is loud and the smell of weed seeps upstairs. He has been told over and over that he is not to smoke dope downstairs. And he still does." How do you change these behaviours of our AKs?

Well, we sure as heck will not be successful telling an AK what to do. We can't use the same tactics we used when our children were young, particularly when our own adult kids are programmed to react to our telling. My wise friend explained in one conversation that her 28-year-old daughter was blown away when she, her mom, started talking to her like an adult. "When I asked her how she thought we might best resolve a certain situation, my daughter giggled, 'Geez, Mom. You just made me feel like I was your co-worker. You want some input into how this might get fixed? That's a change.' And we had a discussion, an adult discussion. Did I have to compromise? Sure, we both did. But we both agreed without a fight."

Being centred in our values allows us to express what we are truly trying to accomplish, what feelings we want to have when a matter is resolved. Sure, we are looking to get some behaviour changed. Why do we want it changed? What is truly bothering us? We want to communicate that end, that intention, to our adult kids. Then the boundaries are clearer. We explain what real end result we are seeking. Does the mom, mentioned earlier, want dope smoking in the basement to stop because she can't stand the smell? Or is she worried about the health of her son's lungs? What button is he pushing? Is he simply disrespectful of the house rules? That's the toughest. "The rule is no smoking dope in the house" lines up with "Don't do it because I told you so," doesn't it? There is a better chance of an agreement when Mom explains her true intentions and reflected values. Even if this mom doesn't get support, at least she has the chance to voice her feeling of being disrespected or her feeling of fear for her son's mental health, whatever is at the root of her caring.

Never Say Never...

Being independent has always been important to me, and we have tried to reinforce this value by expecting our kids to strive for their own independence. And I acknowledge that what I want for them may not be what they want for themselves. That's a little harder to remember. This is my personal foundational value, and it may not be theirs. My attempts at making our AKs independent came in ridiculous statements like: "I will never buy my kids a car." We gave our son my car for a year. "Rent? I am not paying their rent." We paid rent for all three kids while they were at school. Heck, we bought two houses in two different cities so they would have a place to stay, and roommates. Seems I valued my children's comfort more than I valued their independence. Hmmm?

And this is why our conversations with one another as fellow parents are so important. In our wine times, we bounce our stories around and look at ourselves through different lenses. When we share our stories, we leave ourselves vulnerable. We get questioned by friends, "Remember you said you would never…? and here you are doing it." Why did we do exactly what we said we wouldn't do? Something must have held more value and had more meaning. We question ourselves, asking "Did I do the right thing?" And our Sisterhood of Mothers lends us a moment to ponder.

I know now that I can never see any of my children struggle to put a roof over their heads. I will do whatever is possible to give them a home. For them to have their own space is so important to me. It represents to me independence, privacy, and a safe haven. Just how far my desire to provide a home for them will go, I do not know. I do know it would take a lot of discussions before any of them could come home to live with us. And what values does that speak to? What would it take to let them come home to our home? I'm not confident we ever really know how we will react when a difficult time is upon us. These answers might even be formulated at the time of the problem.

The discussions around what we value, and how we choose to live, are tough. We can't deal with our adult children like the high school students who used to live in our home or even the young adults who came and went during post-secondary times. We are not speaking to the same person. Holding our adult kids in the space of being adults, with their own values and principles, will surely allow for more open conversation and healthier relationships.

One father who had experienced the "doing nothing, smoking dope, playing video games" scenario told me his story years ago, before I got this idea to write a book. He told me, "I had to have a serious heart-to-heart at the kitchen table." This dad told his adult son that he worried about his son's future. He worked hard and paid his post-secondary tuition because he wanted his son to find a life where he could support himself and feel pride about his own accomplishments. Maybe even have a family. Dad spilled it all out. He loved his son and wanted his son to be happy, so the behaviour he was witnessing scared him. He wondered if the behaviour was making his son happy.

To cut to the chase, the son confessed his own fears. With no routine now that school was finished, and no job to keep him on track, he had no idea what to do. "Really Gill," the father told me, "he was looking for some boundaries, some routine, some plan of action." And they found it. Of course, it took some time. My adult kids tell me that this young man is doing well now, loving his work, and rocking his accounting world. That warms my heart.

Although our adult kids know us well, they can't always be really sure of what is most important to us. And my new discovery is that we cannot always be sure what is most important to them. Why do we want to spend Christmas together? Why do we want them to stop seeing someone we are afraid has a negative influence? Why do we worry when they hide away in a basement? What if we listened to the request of my inner yogi to find our foundation? And how might our adult kids respond when we come from this place, making communication around the values and principles that are feeling compromised?

Sometimes we can't explain why the hair on the back of our neck stands up or what happened that pushed our button. Sometimes I question why these adult kids baffle or surprise me or make me take pause to wonder about what they could possibly be thinking. And then I breathe. They too are living their life based on their values and what is most important to them at the time. So yes, some of their decisions will be made around their dogs. And we will have to find a way to breathe. Namaste.

15.

The Things We Do… and Don't Do

It is quite mind-blowing the things that my peers and I are doing for their adult kids. I do not exclude myself. I do things for my adult children, after all I am their mother. I like doing things for my kids. Sometimes I just have no idea what they need from me. As moms we have spent many years giving to our children and doing things for our children. These habits are hard to break. But what are we supposed to do for our children as they venture into emerging adulthood? How are we to be as an adult with an adult?

Coming Home

My friend Sarah built an enormous house, giving each adult child a bedroom, and adding a larger space above the garage for more independent living. The house was built when she and her husband were "empty nesters." Their three adult children had all left home. Although two were still in post-grad schools, there were no signs that any of them would return to the nest. Five years later, they have three grandchildren. They also installed a new swimming pool in the backyard this past summer.

Sarah's not from a multi-generational home. There were no circumstances that warranted such planning. Sarah told me she built the home with lots of room to make her grown children always feel welcome. She explained, "We want the kids to bring their families here. I never had that when I was a young mom. Heck, my room became my mom's sewing room the minute I shut the door behind me to go to university." Keeping her AKs feeling welcome was a part of her plan. No one has come home to live, but her AKs do visit often. The bedrooms are a second home for her grown children and families. And the swimming pool is a place of family joy!

Yes, some parents will do over-the-top things, by my measure, for their adult kids. Examples include adding cabins to their property at their cottage or even gifting a down payment for a house. One friend said, "We're giving them their inheritance now so they can use it. This way, I can see it being enjoyed." All great…if you think you will have enough to get yourself through retirement. Sometimes it's the parents who can least afford it who shell out cash to their grown children first. This gifting can be as simple as handing out gas money each time they visit.

One 32-year-old posted on Instagram that his father always leaves a twenty-dollar bill tucked somewhere in his apartment. After each visit the AK finds a twenty behind the coffee maker or in the coffee mug. Cute. He has discovered bills in his medicine cabinet, beside a trophy, and even in the dog's dish!

I am astonished by the number of parents who have reopened their homes to their adult children, and their partners, and their partner's kids. I read the stories parents share on Facebook pages. One woman shared in frustration that she has three AKs living in her home along with their partners and kids. Not a single one of them contributes to rent. One attends school and mom pays full tuition and provides rides to work. Imagine. No one offers her any financial support. She is a single mother, working to ensure her whole family has a roof over their heads. Most of the readers' comments on the page spoke to her about setting timelines and boundaries. Other women were concerned for her own mental health. Clearly, she is a generous woman. In my work, I see many good women who have become victims of their own kindness.

Me? Well, we downsized. Our kids were annoyed, and of course they told us so. Adult children do that. Speak their minds. At least our new house has room for the kids. To visit. Does that make me a bad parent? Or harm our relationship?

Can't Buy Me Love

My friends buy crazy things for their kids, without even asking, or being asked. "I saw this great dresser on the side of the road. It was perfect for my son's front hall, so I loaded it into my van. I took a picture of it for his wife. She didn't want it. She never wants anything I find. I put it outside our house, and it was gone within ten minutes. No harm, no foul." I realised at that moment that my version of being a caring mom does not include a dumpster dive for treasures that nobody really needs. And if my daughter-in-law never liked anything I gave her, I would stop giving her stuff. At least I believe that is how I would behave. That is me, trying to be me. And my friend, she will do her.

My belief is that my adult children can buy their own furniture. Maybe that's because they live so darn far away. Or maybe that is *why* they live so far away. Who knows? But I have always felt we raised our children to become independent adults. To make their own home with their chosen partners. Don't get me wrong, we still *gift* our AKs good stuff. But I don't pick up furniture off the roadside. That just isn't me.

Granny Day Care

One day while my girlfriend Julie and I were travelling out of town, Julie got a phone call. She stepped away to answer. When she came back she shared, "My grandkids are sick today. They have to come home from day care." "That's frustrating for a working mom," I suggested. "Where are the kids then?" Julie is usually their go-to babysitter. "Their dad had to come home from work to stay with them. His parents couldn't take the kids because they had things to do. *Things to do,*" she repeated with air quotes. "Who can't go and get their grandkids? What kind of *'things to do'* keeps a grandparent away from their grandchildren? I mean," she continued, "what kind of grandparent does that?"

I am pretty sure I am the kind of grandparent that will do that. Remember, I do not have any grandchildren, so I don't really know. But I am pretty sure that if I have *things to do*, I think I will want to do those things. Let the dad get home to look after the sick children. Will I be a bad grandparent, or parent, for thinking that? As a grandma, does my role include being an on-call sitter?

These are the questions we ask ourselves. What do our adult children expect from our relationship? We can never ask this too many times. This is the quandary of these years. How do we transition into a new, less responsible parent? These are the issues that make this Parent-AK relationship so confusing and trying. Surprising to me. I thought all these choices would be clear. To me, and to them.

Giving Joyfully

Parents of adult kids will find what suits them best. Not overnight, but with some trial and error. Some will give their adult children the shirt off their back. *And I am not sure how well that will go over when some naked 62-year-old is running free.* What does the consequence look like to parents who still give and give and give some more? Are these parents happy? Are they making up for some lost opportunity of being a better parent when the kid was younger? Are they still doing that weighty guilt thing? I made a conscious effort to quit guilt long ago.

Not all the moms who shared their stories are happy with their giving situation. I get that. But what would happen if we gave only that which we can give freely and joyfully? There are parents who resent their adult children for what has been given to them. Parents who gave when they were not asked to give. Parents who do not feel appreciated. Do we want our relationships with our AKs to be like that?

Experts caution parents on enabling their children versus allowing for growth and independence. When the kids were little, we held their hands as they learned to walk. And then we let go. Like taking off the trainers on the bicycle. We parents are there until the skill is learned and the child can take off independently. Letting go is so hard, yet so rewarding when you see the smiles of accomplishment.

For years, my friend and I have discussed the fact that many parents convince themselves they are doing something for their kids when really, their hearts are fed by the act of giving. They love to give to their kids. Nothing wrong with that. We can admire their generous nature. But what if the parents become resentful of this constant gifting? What will happen when the AKs don't give any appreciation for what is given? Giving too much, or receiving too much, may breed guilt and resentment for both our AKs and for us, too. "I didn't ask for that Mom. Please take it back," or, "I told you to stop giving stuff to my kids (meaning grandkids)." My friends have shared those stories. Oh, finding that balance is not easy! Sometimes we may have to recognize that we are pleasing ourselves by the giving.

Enabling?

I wonder if by assisting regularly, we are inadvertently sending a message to our AKs that they are not competent? Sometimes that's how the giving might be received. And I can't believe how much parents are still giving...to their much older AKs...like the 30-plus AKs. Are we killing their confidence? Some research says *yes*.

One scientist studying emerging adults offered up this idea. The more an adult child is working towards a goal, the more a parent of the adult child might offer support and assistance. On the flip side, if an adult child is doing nothing toward a goal, the parent is only being used, and perhaps enabling their Adult Kid. Seems silly if the parents are working on the goal alone.

There are parents who can get their AKs jobs. I didn't think it was possible, but I know some who have done just that. Our local plumber has his son taking over his business. After he did all the work to become a certified plumber. One other friend bought the lawn care equipment necessary for their AKs to operate a summer lawn care business. Another retired but working part-time friend was chatting with a customer and as a bit of a joke offered up his daughter as a worker. The customer took him seriously and hired the daughter. Seems Dad played headhunter by accident. Most parents can't do that. Some parents might not want to be involved in job-hunting. But if a business opportunity suits a child and allows the business to stay in the family, wouldn't that be a good scenario? Allowing for independence, of course, and given a transition period for teaching and advising and mentoring.

If we don't have a business as a teaching tool, how are we teaching financial planning and sound budgeting? Some of my friends, and okay maybe me, continue to pay for cell phones, Netflix, car insurance, groceries, or home renovations. That's just it: in some cases we aren't teaching or helping. We are *enabling* our adult children to rely on us. They gradually become entitled. I am uncomfortable with that word, but it could be true. I am guilty as charged in many respects.

You Do You, But Mindfully

One idea I just heard discussed on a Mel Robbins podcast is the difference between "being used" and being in a situation everyone is "used to." What if our children are not changing their behaviours, not moving out of the basement, not applying for work, not paying their own bills, because they are used to having all of that taken care of for them? Perhaps it is just as easy for them to not do it for themselves, because it is all being managed anyway. Why bother? That resonates with me. What might I do that I continue to do that is enabling them to remain dependent? I do operate their Canadian bills and bank accounts. Does that make me too tied to them?

On the other side, many parents set tight boundaries around what they financially and materially give to their adult children. One set of parents I know, who are highly paid, chose not to contribute to their child's post-grad professional education. Not one cent. That's a serious "goodbye" as their AK headed off to student loans as big as mortgages! But this is where those parents set the limits, boundaries around their behaviour.

I so admire that this discussion was held before the situation existed. The AKs understood that parental financing stopped after one degree in their educational journey. "Our kids always knew we would support them for one postsecondary degree or certificate. Everything else was on them." Are these adult kids financially independent? Yes, they are! Do they have mega student loans? Yes, they do. But they manage. And both parents and AKs are fine with this arrangement. That seems to be the goal. To be in full communication about expectations and boundaries.

"You do you" when it comes to giving to the adult children. I have to remind myself of this. I try to stay aware of those nasty "competition" and "comparison" bugs. Yes, even as adults we fall into these traps. We can feel guilty, embarrassed, awkward, and boastful about what we give our own adult kids. None of these are productive emotions. We have to live with the consequences of all our giving, and lack thereof. We, as parents, have to do what keeps us sane and comfortable. We want to make decisions about what we give based on how we feel in our giving and how our offers will be received. Not to mention stay within the financial limitations available. The decisions we make when we go against our own values, those are the difficult ones. Those decisions can elicit anger, frustration, and weakened relationships. Maybe it's best if we just act according to what we are willing to accept. Being inauthentic affects our own anxiety, guilt, and stress. "You do you" is how I choose to guide my giftings. Cheers to that.

16.

Boundaries

One hot summer day, Julie and I were chatting about Christmas plans. Julie also has three adult kids, the youngest 27 years old. It seems we both tread lightly around certain issues with certain children. We each have one child who doesn't like to be asked about their future plans. We tiptoe around the subject when we want to ask them what their immediate future holds. The boundaries of our conversations were arbitrarily set by us when we learned the consequences of asking too many questions.

Zip It

Teasingly Julie slid two fingers across her lips, like she was zipping them up. "Maybe we should do this at times. When that certain topic has been opened, we might need to 'zip it'." We both giggled. "Yeah, that's a good one," I agreed. Her other signal is moving her hand horizontally in front of her body, making a division line, a fence, a boundary. "Jeff and I use this sign when we are on the phone or Facetiming the kids. It's our way of reminding each other 'don't cross that line in conversation' or 'don't open that door.'" "Maybe if we didn't cross the line," I suggested, "we wouldn't have to 'zip it.'"

If you are a parent of adult kids, you might want to learn these signals to zip it and draw the line. And use them. There will be times when saying less or nothing at all will be better for the relationship. I am reminded of the podcast entitled "Bite Your Tongue." There are times when it is best to leave some things unsaid. "Zipping it" takes practice, practice, practice.

We are trying to navigate the seas of parenting/not parenting our adult kids. Trying not to drive the boat into turbulent storms. I am convinced these are not uncharted waters. It's just that no one I know has shared a well-marked map. Goodness knows parents are discussing these issues with one another. What do we say, and what do we leave unsaid? It's a balancing act.

Frustrated with the uncut lawn at her daughter's new home, Sheila confided in me, "The two of them have no time for this home. Lawn cutting is beyond them. The back-door lightbulb burned out last week and it is yet to be replaced. They use their cell phones for light! How long can they do that?" Ironically, one of our next conversations began, "The kids are selling their house. They have decided they are not 'homeowners.'"

I guess Sheila wasn't the only one who saw the uncut lawn and the burned-out light. Sometimes, it pays to 'zip it' and wait. She saved an argument there. Whew. And if she had opened the discussion about home owning, would she have strengthened the relationship? Of course not. Hm. Think before we speak.

Pick Your Battles

When my children were young, my mantra was "pick your battles." Barbara Colorosso, the Backbone parent supporter, coached parents to ask themselves, "Am I willing to allow my child to face the natural and logical consequences?" If it is not life threatening or morally threatening, then let them have the experience. Maybe I should revive all these mantras and guidelines for life with adult children. When the kids were younger, we had experts and textbooks and lots of resources. Now I have wine chats.

Please do not take this personally: our generation, at times, can be stuck in set ideas and mindsets. There are studies on growth versus fixed mindsets and I have learned I grew up with pretty fixed or set patterns of beliefs. In life, we always do our best to live within our fixed mindsets. That keeps us balanced. A dirty kitchen is a sign of laziness. A freshly made bed is the only way to start the day. Good neighbours mow their lawns. I believed people are either born artistic or they aren't, and I wasn't, so why try? I had set beliefs around the silliest things. Perhaps you have recognized some of your set beliefs and deemed them unimportant or irrelevant and let them go. You may discover these beliefs as you examine your values. Perhaps you are in the process of recognizing set beliefs you still hold that have no truth at all. Hmm.

Last month a dad said to me, referring to his adult daughter and husband, "Can you believe they painted the woodwork in the dining room? Painted that beautiful rich oak, they did. What were they thinking?" Luckily, he did not mention to his kids his belief that wood should never be painted. His mindset and belief were pretty dated. But seriously, what difference does it make to him or them? This decorating battle changes sides every couple of decades. Commenting on that doesn't help the future relationship building. At all.

Sitting at a swimming pool, my friend's daughter commented on her six-month-old's tangled mop of hair. "Until she is about five years old, I won't ever cut her hair," said the 30-year-old first-time mom. Without skipping a beat, my friend, the child's grandma stated, "Oh yes you will." Don't you think I should have given her the 'zip it' sign? A comment like that could have led to a discussion requesting Mom butt out or mind her business. Is it worth it? I think we would all agree on one answer.

Learning To Stay Quiet

I remember when I first learned the power of remaining quiet. My good friend's daughter had moved in with a fellow who happened to deal drugs for his day job. He was a handsome biker, a real catch for a girl who had just quit university and was making an attempt at rebelling and making some noise! Kristi was in love with her "bad boy."

Kristi was in love and broke. And Kristi was at that stage when her love life was her highest priority. Her phone calls home were pleas for money and then cursing at her parents when she was refused. "Come by for some groceries. Anything in the kitchen is yours for the taking." Kristi was not driving home for food. No way.

What she did drive home for was the family van. The boyfriend's motorbike was not taking her to work regularly, so she needed some wheels of her own. And the family van was usually what she drove when she lived at home. Or some such reasoning. Anyway, Kristi visited one night and stole the van.

"Honestly, she had to have done a ten-point turn to get that van out of our laneway," her mom sighed. "It was parked right against the garage door in front of Bob's car. I have no idea how she did that!" We laughed at her determination. But seriously, we were worried. This guy had charm. Kristi was smitten.

"Don't press charges," was the advice of a family friend and registered psychotherapist. "Ask her why she felt she had to take the van without asking. Remind her that what she did is a punishable theft. Then set some terms you feel comfortable with. And stick to them. But do not take any measures out of anger. Make sure she knows she is a loved member of your family."

It was so hard to watch as Kristi dug herself deeper into debt and more serious law-breaking activity. Her mom and dad really had to work to zip it and set boundaries. Those boundaries were set for the good of both their adult child and them.

My friends, Bob and Amy, held their ground. Lots of welcoming Kristi home when she was ready. Lots of invitations for her to come for dinner or join in the family vacation. Without the boyfriend. They remained firm about that. With apologies. "We know you love him Kristi, but we do not right now. Maybe one day we will see what you see." Bob and Amy became experts in "zipping it." And Kristi came home. To open arms. Without her biker friend.

What Will Those Words Sound Like Ten Years From Now?

Esther Goetz, an author, blogger and writer of Moms of Bigs, had an interesting prompt. "Think of the long game." When we react to one specific situation we are focused on the here and now, thinking only of ourselves and our emotional reaction. If we can muster the energy to breathe, pause, and think of the long game, we may find the courage and strength to be more curious, more patient, more empathetic and see beyond the moment. What reaction will be best for the relationship we want to hold into the future? I can see value in that thinking.

There are definitely conversations we as parents of adult kids share with one another, and not our children. Let's start with the ones that begin: They never should have…Couldn't they have…Wouldn't it have been easier to…We can be warned against those tricky and destructive phrases: woulda, coulda, shoulda, when chatting with our own adult kids. They keep us in the here and now and do not prepare us for a strong future connection.

Remember, our adult kids are not making decisions independently all the time. They have partners, roommates, in- laws, and spouses. They have Instagram advice, Facebook, Tik Tok, Twitter and Google. They have a team to assist with decision making and sometimes they will add us to the team. Other times we may be cut. All boundaries, theirs and ours, are worth respecting. Let's recognize and respect their boundary line, while thinking of the long game.

The Long Game

Balancing when to speak up and when to zip it is one thin tightrope walk. Even the experts take the time to chat about this balance. Sadly for them, there is no wine. Dr. Ellen Braaten and Denise Gorant, hosts of the podcast "Bite Your Tongue," interviewed Dr. Ruth Nemzoff, author of the book *Don't Bite Your Tongue: How to Foster Rewarding Relationships with Your Adult Children*. Hearing the two sides was enlightening. They agreed that there are times for both response types. The podcast hosts named their podcast with a catchy title, and a lot of tongue-in-cheek. Neither host nor guest believes parents should always bite their tongues or always speak their minds.

The book author shared advice and suggestions around staying open and in full communication with adult children. Dr. Nemzoff is against walking on eggshells and always keeping your opinions to yourself. She offered up tools for better discussions. She pushed proactive openness with early boundary setting and balancing the conversations for both parties to speak. "The injunctions to 'bite your tongue', 'zip your lip' 'be quiet', and 'don't say anything,' frustrate us. We have things to say, opinions to share… in a way that won't lead to a screaming fight or an abruptly ended phone call."

Both host and author believe that boundaries need to be set. Just state what the boundaries are. Don't hide them from one another. When Bob and Amy said, "We are not ready to welcome your partner into our house. Yet." they stood their ground and left space for a change of heart. That's a skilled response. I had better practise that, too!

I do know there may be decisions our AKs make that are unbearable for us. Maybe we just can't take it anymore. The consequences of our AKs actions may be both morally and life threatening. Many young AKs have left the house with a partner who does not have a positive influence. Like Kristi's biker boy, some partners lure AKs into worlds of crime. Parents are entitled and invited to state they are worried, fear for their AKs future, and would prefer another alternative. But we all know the consequences of threats, ultimatums, and bribes. No one wins. No one learns. No one is happy.

My brother-in-law introduced me to the show Breaking Bad. I was hooked. Even on the small screen, men broached the subject of being a parent to adult daughters. "What do you do to support them?" asked a character hunched over a bar, beer in hand. "Love them," answered the other. "Even though you want to shake them and tell them exactly what to do?" "Yes. Love them." That scene was made even more significant as, unbeknownst to the men, one of the adult daughters was lying dead of a drug overdose. We see it on our televisions and of course in real life. Parents are talking about how to love their children when they are grown. What if they are making horrific choices? How do we stop our adult kids when we are confident their decisions are bad?

Then, my question to myself is this: How badly do I want to keep the relationship with my adult child? Do I want a bit of a bruised ego and a solid relationship, or do I want to be heard and increase the possibility of losing the ties with my AKs? What good can we do if our adult children won't talk or listen to us? I guess it is up to us to know what really matters to us. And again, I think focusing on the long game will be a stance I practise.

Boundaries are not intended to be fierce. They are loving and firm. When we forget this, we are either too loving and we try to please and make up for something, or we are too firm and it comes across as judgemental. We want balance.

-Jennifer Williams, Heartmanity.com

The Friendly Neighbour

Our AKs have beliefs and opinions and responsibilities. They do have a method of decision making. Their processes may make them reach other results, different than we would have chosen for them. How do we relax and remember that when the student is ready, the teacher will appear? We can't push that teachable moment. Those moments happen naturally. If we push them, we do more harm. Unsolicited advice is never welcome, and is often perceived as an insult, or a lack of faith in our children. When I sent my son some job postings I had seen in LinkedIn, he sent me a reply email. "Do you think I don't know where to look for work? I know how. And I will find something. You don't have to do it with me." Bam. Trying to be helpful without being asked can be so damaging.

It seems to me, to summarise the advice I have received, the best way to communicate with our adult children is to step aside, support, and stay quiet until asked. That zip it thing again. Relax and watch them do their best and see what they know. Or ask questions about what they know. Save yourself. Save your relationship. Stop trying to fix it. Show self restraint. Say sorry. Show support by loving them. Listen. All easier said than done. But all doable.

Some of the best advice I was offered came from a physician friend. He was only stepping in the front door to drop off a letter and made the error of asking, "How are you doing?" Thirty minutes later our conversation turned to his suggestion: "Have you ever tried treating your adult child like a friendly neighbour? Pretend you are talking over the fence. You like them, but you aren't going to comment when they rip out their garden. Imagine if a conversation with a neighbour went like this: 'What the heck? What were you thinking? Did you not think about how expensive it is going to be to replace the flowers in the area? Do you know the cost of growing grass in its place? Why on earth would you do that? You should have just left it.' Nope. No one would want to be spoken to that way."

You get the idea. I love this perspective. And I do want to be friends with my adult kids. I can see how this lens has value in the times of differences, the days of complicated relationships. Using this "neighbour" treatment might just help with setting boundaries. Don't say what you wouldn't say to a neighbour. How we as parents manage this balance of leaning in, helping, offering support, and butting out, staying curious, and observing in a neutral state, will differ with time and certainly with circumstances. No doubt, some adult children get into serious situations and life-threatening times. In those more dire times, families need more support than a conversation over wine with friends. No need to exclude your friend relationships, just add a professional therapist. And we need to look after ourselves to be strong enough to weather the storm.

In our relationships with our friends, we zip it and we set boundaries. At least I know I do. Some friends are just more open to challenging discussions. The zip-it mode of communication is not disrespectful; in fact, I think it's just the opposite. We are trying to honour the choices our adult children make without being critics. I like that. And boundaries? Once we acknowledge them, I bet they can be very useful. I am practising for the long game.

> *What if all our big kid's bad choices will be weaved into their story so that when it comes down to it, they end up on a "good" path, the one that's theirs alone to take?*
>
> -MOMS OF BIGS, esterjoygoetz.com

17.

Serious Troubles

Let me start with an apology. I am sorry. I apologize for my sometimes flippant attitude about troublesome adult children situations. I know some parents and adult children have serious, traumatic experiences. Issues may not be as simple and straightforward as having an AK ask you to use genderless language or stop buying pink dresses for your granddaughter. Sometimes, concerns and worries with our adult children are very serious. I acknowledge that poor mental health, addictions, and on- going physical and developmental issues require a whole book. This is not that book. But, I would be remiss if we didn't spend a few pages taking a look at really, really tough circumstances. We all know someone who is living them. To them, I raise a glass.

Our Loud Inner Noises

Have you ever watched a movie without the sound? Especially one of the thrilling, scary scenes when the victims are about to get attacked, jumped or killed? Without the sound, the whole scary thing is easier, less frightening. We can focus clearly on the action, by taking away the fear. Silencing our minds allows space for clearer, more rational thinking and less emotional responses.

Life has a soundtrack. Our noisiest and most habitual soundtrack is the voice in our heads. Our thoughts. Only the most practiced can quiet them. Meditation practises, or following the breath are just some methods of silencing the noise. Our thoughts are particularly loud and distracting in the silence of the night. They can be deafening. There is no volume or mute button that has an immediate fix. That's why people meditate or take drugs or turn music on. We search for the still and the quiet or try to numb disturbing thoughts. Our inner soundtrack can be changed. It is not easy, but it can be done.

If we do not control this voice inside, it can change the capacity of what we are able to do in a day. With too much noise, our memories fail; we create untrue stories; our reality is twisted or unclear. Sometimes the mind is so loud we become physically ill. Our hearts and our guts reel with discomfort.

As parents we may experience this noisy, out-of-rhythm soundtrack when our adult children are disrespectful, lethargic, unmotivated or themselves quite tormented. Our worries for them can become the loudest, most blaring sounds. Most likely, their soundtracks are equally disturbing to them. Think about that for a minute. Our adult children may be just or even more distressed than us.

When Jennifer's 25-year-old son came home broke and jobless, he spent all his days playing video games in the basement. I cannot count the number of times I have been told of this scenario. Jennifer shared, "I lie awake and worry.

How can I help him? What can I possibly do? And then I try to think of all the things I might assist with and end up imagining him saying 'NO' to everything." I could only muster a nod in response.

"My sleeplessness makes me more tired and irritated with him when I wake. And the cycle of yelling and arguing gets worse. I can't imagine how badly he feels about himself. And his circumstances. Clearly, I am not helping."

Finding Help

Requests, discussions, or simple questions to your adult child can turn into loud, angry fights, verbal and in some cases, physical. There are ways to find help and support. Our friendship groups are a safe place to start talking. Professionals are better resources to tap. Not alcohol or recreational drugs. Certainly not the time to drink more wine. Real professional help, which might include meditation, therapy, prescriptions. We need to turn the volume down before we can change the soundtrack. There has to be a fade, a cut, a tempo change into a new, more relaxed soundtrack.

Professional counselling or therapy can be expensive. But there are resources available through family doctors and local clinics. Support groups exist, especially for addictions and now online support groups, Facebook groups are available to share resources and information and support. Just google any parent- adult child issue: estrangement, defiant adult children, disrespectful adult children, addiction, drug abuse. Lots of support and resources are offered. Check them out before you dive too deeply.

Lifelong support

Some children have special needs right from birth. Children with physical conditions that will never change, cerebral palsy, muscular dystrophy, cystic fibrosis, Down's Syndrome, seizure disorders, or other permanent challenges. These parents have such tough decisions and choices to make with and for their adult children. Often expensive choices need to be made as parents age and seek to have their adult children left in good hands.

Amy has a child with Fragile X syndrome. Similar to Down's Syndrome, as I understand the disease and the child. He is an amazing adult. People love him. His parents are aging. They are seeking a place for their son to live more independently of them. At one time they were looking into buying a house and bringing other adult children into the home and hiring a worker to live there also. Quite an expense, so he is still at home. They continue to look for suitable programmed housing. Such a worry that will not go away.

Another 30-year-old adult I know, works as an accountant. She lives with cerebral palsy. Her life is in a wheelchair with full support for all the needs of her quadriplegia. Her parents are over 70 years old. Her physical needs are demanding. She is not. Imagine having to find a residence for a smart, hilarious, hardworking woman who has high physical needs? My hope is that there are plenty of resources for adult children who are still very much a part of their parents' lives. I hope so. But I am not confident.

The Unexpected

I never thought about any of these scenarios when we were deciding to have children. Not once. My positive Pollyanna self, dreamed of holding a healthy, happy child who would find bumps and bruises and bangs, then get back up and laugh. My head never went to a place of addictions, job losses, financial struggles, physical ailments, or early death. Suicide even.

These are the surprises that are horrific, life altering shocks. Situations that are devastating, debilitating, difficult. Beyond words. With our glass of wine, we talk of these happenings, too. We consider ways we can help, things we can do to ease pains, how we might gently offer opportunities for those parents to talk, without being nosy or rude. These conversations are part of life as a parent of adults. I wish they weren't.

My darling has been known to say, "If we didn't have children, what would we worry about?" I wonder. Nothing in life matters as much as our children, regardless of their ages.

I had to include this chapter. I am saddened that parents have to face these issues and problems, but these life situations are real. The cashier at the grocery store, or the woman in line ahead of you, they may be facing these tough adult children issues in their lives. We just never know what trials people are living with. But if you know a family who has adult children, chances are good there have been tough moments, tough days, tough years. In remembering this, perhaps we will find it easier to zip it, to set healthy boundaries, to communicate openly and with respect. Preventative medicine perhaps. Or maybe just being mindful that these adults are the children we love.

18.

We've Got This

One Australian mom I recently met told me that she was feeling so good about where she was in this moment of time with her adult children and their lives. All three AKs were enjoying their work, making plans for their futures with positivity, and her life felt just as good. Her sense of contentment was warming for me. There was peacefulness in what she spoke. Her pride was evident, and her joy was palpable, contagious even.

Was the life for her children always this smooth? Of course not. Does she acknowledge there will be some future bumps and surprises? She does. Her AKs live all over the world. She knows it will not always be so calm, but her acceptance of them as adults making their own decisions was so clear to me.

Her happiness was not dependent upon that of her children. She accepted that they are now all adults. "They will make their own decisions, won't they?" She meant this so genuinely.

Another long-time friend is totally amazed that all three of her children live right in our hometown. She had no expectations that would happen. She had no designs. But here she is today experiencing life with one family down the road, one within walking distance, and another a short drive away. Four grandchildren and three happy families. Does she hope for a spouse for one unmarried child? Of course. Does she go out looking for one? Absolutely not. Is every moment of her day consumed with the assumed loneliness of her AK? No. She has confidence this adult will find their way. It's their life now.

And sad scenarios exist. The families who have lost adult children to drugs and suicide. The parents watching an adult child struggle with mental health issues and addictions. The mom who never speaks to her adult daughter and cannot meet her grandchildren. I get that not all life situations can be rosy. But if we as parents of adult kids are holding on to the planning, directing, instructing, demanding parts of parenting, perhaps we are lessening our own lives and the lives of our adult children.

Our Own Happiness

Is it possible to get to a place where our family does not determine our happiness, our contentment? Maybe. As mothers of adults, we do not have to be as happy as our least happy child. Some of our adult kids will eff up. They will make stupid decisions, make illogical moves in life. And many won't. Thank goodness for family, friends, groups, and therapists that will support us as we love our adult kids. Appreciation to those who will sit and drink wine and engage in discussions. Life is better shared.

When I first started writing this book, I asked friends to submit stories about their experiences with their own AKs. Most of my friends laughed and told me that I already knew their stories. Cute. But not really accurate. I knew what they had chosen to share in our times over books, cards, wine, ski lifts. The private struggles were still private. "No," they told me. "You do know. Maybe you forgot, but we shared. How do you think we got through those times?" What I heard at that time, and what I hear now at the conclusion of my writing is this: there are references to "getting through" and "moving on". I didn't hear that initially. We all have selective hearing. When I first heard the other stories, my focus was on the issues, the problems, what was tough, confusing and baffling about life with AKs. My ears weren't open to hearing that there is change and growth and, therefore, hope. What I have observed is there is very little we can contribute now, except love, listening, patience, and the offer of assistance, not pushing.

Endings…

One dear friend, Mary, took the time to write me heartfelt emails. Her first email was a quick, "While I was out with Joan, we discussed your book idea. Neither of us have troubles or struggles with our adult children. I was thinking that, and Joan confirmed. We were out paddling in Algonquin Park without a care in the world." Not a direct quote but close. Then I got this email, which I asked permission to share in direct quotes. Mary agreed.

"The answer to your questions about life with AKs may depend upon perspective and history. I don't recall exactly how much you know about my boys, but I had a great number of worries about them for many different reasons over the years." Mary explained to me the medical heart surgeries they faced with their first born and the later issues around a learning disability he had. She told the tales of teen bullying and more physical illnesses. And yet, this son "went on to earn both a university degree and a college diploma, has his own successful business, a wonderful wife, two wonderful daughters, a beautiful home, and he's happy and healthy. So, do I worry about him? No, I really don't."

Wow. There were plenty of causes for worry and concern through the early years and the teen years, and even into his twenties. His second decade of life was a period of growing confidence as this son found his way and found a girlfriend, now wife, to share his life. His early history was not good. My friend and her husband had to support his issues for a long time. Thank goodness for happy endings. Today I hear stories of Mary loving her little granddaughters and sharing many happy times with this son and his wife. Her joy brings me joy.

The part of the story that Mary left out of her email, maybe on purpose, is that she has a second son. A son who experienced a long battle with depression and anxiety throughout his twenties. She is a saint. He gave her many sleepless nights and worrisome visits to doctors' offices and hospitals. Somehow, we forget and forgive the times we stress over medical issues. That health issue was resolved for her son, who is in a happy relationship with stepchildren who love and respect him. Mary was very stressed for many years. And here she is, paddling without care. And taking extended ski trips. Yes. There is a light!

Tips And Tools

For now, let's reflect, even including a listy thing, on the tips and tools we might employ as we build our adult-adult relationships with our own children.

I wish someone would have told me that the hardest part of parenting is the work I would have to do on myself.

-Insta post @Momwell (Formerly Happy as a Mother)

Knowing ourselves, our hidden and obvious expectations, and our own set of values and principles is all a part of learning who we are. And we are evolving, changing humans, so the discovery is ongoing. The way we can surprise ourselves in these later years of life is a gift. This is wisdom. How can "you do you" unless you actually know "you?" Now that our children are adults, we can focus on ourselves and our actions, interactions, and behaviours with a new insight. We are building adult-adult relationships, different with each child. Our decisions will be made with the long game in mind. Our mature selves allow us to be humble and listen if we want to continue a relationship that, remember, is more important to us than it is to them.

Our Sisterhood of Mothers is a very supportive, bright group. Often, we can come up with some insights that are new and revealing. My favourite research moments were when some expert, author or researcher, or podcast host, Instragrammer, or Facebook page cited just what we wine- sharing friends had discovered in our chats. There are times to bite your tongue, zip it, times to set boundaries, and times to respect the boundaries that have been set for us. Yes, we are in a bit of a balancing act.

Meeting our adult children where they are at, and not where we hoped, dreamed, envisioned, or even thought they would be, is key to finding the flow, the rhythm of the relationship. Listening will allow us to know that spot. Listening will bring us to the space of empathy and open conversation. Whether we choose to be friends or friendly will matter only in the moment. Each moment brings its own meeting point. Communication is the key to every relationship. And communication starts with finding the space to listen, a place of curiosity versus judgment. Whether your physical space is a formally declared family round table, an impromptu phone call, or a scheduled Zoom chat, our times of interacting will determine the nature of the relationship.

Expectations can get in our way of clear communication. Unless we open ourselves to examine what our expectations were or are. Or understand what expectations our adult children have of us. Self-knowledge can be challenging. But it is surprising, even to me in my coaching life, how much of ourselves we don't know, until we know. What are those blind spots? What patterns of thought or behaviour are repeating and coming back to jeopardize relationships or thwart communication? Thank goodness for wine chats with good friends and professional sessions when the going is really tough. Those meetups provide insight, ideas, suggestions, and some new tools.

Perhaps your children are in their early twenties and their journey in this emerging adult stage is just beginning. Maybe you are on the other side and now entering the adult-adult time of life with your children. Wherever you are, may you find the support and resources right where you are. Maybe we can be a little more vulnerable knowing we are not alone. This stage in life is real and we can thrive, right here. You've got this! You are not alone.

Lift your glass and salute. Here's to this moment,
Cheers, Gill

Tools And Strategies (The Listy Thing)

Listen
Be a Friend
Stay curious
Set boundaries
Respect boundaries
Validate feelings
Zip It
Bite Your Tongue
Identify expectations
Think of the LONG game
Know the cost of your opinions
Hold family round table meetings
Meet together for shared interest activities
Seek professional help when needed or suggested
Be vulnerable with friends, groups and associates
Accept you don't know what you don't know
Know your Principles and Values
You Do You

About the Author

Gill (Jill) Tillmann lives in Orillia, Ontario, Canada with her husband. No dogs or cats. Their children are citizens of the world and currently live in three different countries. No one is in Canada. Either Gill and her husband did something great as parents, or something terribly wrong. They will own either, and both!

As a high school teacher, and a life coach, Gill spent many hours with adults, teens and grads as they worked to build their plans for their futures. Her curiousity about the continued struggles for her own AKs, other parents and 'emerging adults' is what motivated the writings in this book.

During the final stages of writing this book, Gill and her husband became grandparents! She loves the joys of change and growth and continues her journey of self-discovery, now as a Grandmother.

Gill can be reached at gilltillmann@gmail.com.

Praise for Pour the Wine

◆ ◆ ◆

In each chapter, Gill takes you on a wonderful journey of the shared experiences we have with our adult children. Many stories are funny and insightful, other are courageous and heartfelt. All are about real life in today's world. The story may not be exactly the same as yours, but they will make you think and certainly prompt deeper discussions… maybe even some self-reflection.

NIKKI DERSNAH, MOTHER OF 3 ADULT CHILDREN

Gill Tillmann, the author and also my sister-in-law, has put together a thoughtful, insightful and helpful guide for the "Boomer and Gen X Parents" trying to understand and be helpful to this "confusing and complicated and wonderful" generation of Adult Kids.

As a parent of two adult children, a trained individual and family therapist, and a family physician, I commend Gill's dive into what can be a complicated and heart wrenching time of life. Discuss this easy- to- read book with your partner and your friends. Perhaps lend a copy to your own Adult Kid to get their input. Sit back, struggle and enjoy!

DR. MARY PAT TILLMANN, MSW, MD, CCFP-FCFP

A candid and relatable read for anyone that has adult children. The author's narrative voice is comforting and humorous, providing pearls of wisdom and advice that give color to the many emotions that go along with this phase of life. Both thought-provoking and inspirational, I would recommend sharing the book with friends, setting a date to discuss it, serving some wine and then simply bond over the life experiences that most families share throughout the generations. Connecting with people over conversation about the topics in this book is likely to be a heartwarming and eye-opening experience for all.

LAURA ZUKOSKY, MOTHER OF FOUR ADULT CHILDREN, AND AUTHOR OF THE BOOK, "WE'RE NOT HERE FOR THE HOCKEY. A GUIDE TO RAISING A COMPETITIVE ATHLETE WITHOUT GOING NUCKING FUTS."

Resources

Start with some of these sources. You may find just what you need in this moment.

Instagram
@respectfulmom @Momwell
@MomsofBigs
@kimmuenchparentcoach @sallyharriscoach
@pamtronsoncoaching @motherofinfluence
@never_empty_nest

Books
Don't Bite Your Tongue by Dr. Ruth Nemzoff
Emerging Adults by Jeffery Jensen Arnett
You and Your Adult Child: How to Grow Together in Challenging Times by Laurence Steinberg
Doing Life With Your Adult Children by Jim Burns
Emotional Agility by Susan David

Websites
Heartmanity.com | Jennifer Williams
ParentsLettingGo.com | Jeffrey Arnett
SSEA.org | Society for The Study of Emerging Adulthood
RealLifeParentingGuide.com | Kim Muench

Podcasts

Bite Your Tongue, Building Relationships with Your Adult Child
Adultescence: A Podcast for Post Grads
Mel Robbins: especially Episode "You Learn This Too Late"

Articles

"Altogether Now" by Amy Maclin in *Simple Living Magazine*

Discussion Guide

Chapter 1: Beyond The Empty Nest

What kind of parent do you hope, plan to be with your adult children?

What do these adult kids want from us and how do we deliver?

When your friends get together does the topic of conversation come around to adult children naturally? Why do you think that is?

Chapter 2: Research Evidence That We Are Not Alone!

The definition of "emerging" adult includes a stage of: exploration, self- focused thinking, feeling in-between, and seeing possibilities. Do you recognize your adult children having these experiences? Maybe some of your adult child's behaviour is really a symptom of one of those descriptors. Describe how this might be true with one of your adult children.

Research shows our adult children are less interested in our relationship than we are. Do you believe this is a good thing?

Chapter 3: Their Journey To Find Themselves

How could a parent hold any expectation or prepare for such turns in life as adult children being gay, or choosing a gender change?

How do you weigh your values, perhaps religious based, against your child's needs?

Chapter 4: What's Their Work?

Some sources are quoting as many as 15 job changes for this generation. "Job hopping is the new normal." What are your feelings and experience around this fact.

What has surprised you most about how this generation makes a living?

Have you ever found yourself aware of your expectations getting in the way of your relationship? What can we do to ease this tension?

Chapter 5: Next Chapter…Love Life

How do we step aside or be less worried for the unmarried state of our children?

What reasons might there be to actually worry and fret about an adult child's relationship? How can we support them, without becoming a part of their issue?

Quite often we observe our adult children and we just "don't get it". Do we need to understand?

Chapter 6: Not All Nests Are Empty

The family 'round table' discussion was a new concept for me. We do this around vacation planning, but not around living together. How might such a formalized conversation work in your household?

How do we cope with living together with an adult child? Or an adult child and their significant others?

Chapter 7: You're Seeing Who?

When do we step in and when do we sit back? Are there some general guidelines or rules you follow?

Chapter 8: French Tucks And Other Lessons

"We might just walk on eggshells so as not to ruffle feathers." Why is that? What do we fear? How can we and they offer suggestions without being opinionated and critical?

Chapter 9: Sibling Rivalry

How and when will you break off all financial ties with your adult children? For the contributions you do make, how do you determine fair and equal?

And which is more important to you? Fair or equal? In what ways might you treat one child differently from another?

Chapter 10: Can We Be Friends?

Are you hoping to be, or are you already 'friends' with your adult child? What does 'friendship' look like in a parent/AK relationship?

Some believe unsolicited advice may be construed as criticism. Do you have a time this happened? How does that change the relationship at that moment? How can you make an apology or resolution?

Chapter 11: Holidays and Other Get-togethers

How have your family traditions changed?

How have you encouraged input and assistance around family holidays and celebrations?

Is your behaviour different when you are a guest at your AKs home? How? And Why?

Chapter 12: Maybe Baby

What stories or situations have surprised you the most about being a grandparent?

There will be expectations you and your children have regarding the role of grandparent. What expectations might you consider changing, broadening, or deleting?

What surprises have you seen as our AKs prepare for parenthood or for childlessness?

Chapter 13: Dangerous Expectations...

Have you stopped to think about your expectations of your AK? Now might be a good time to make a quick list of your expectations. Just brainstorm.

Let them flow! You might get a surprise.

What expectations do you believe your AKs have of you? Are you brave enough to ask them?

Chapter 14: Values, Foundation, Grounding

We are still learning about ourselves – and changing at the same time, as we are being parents of adult kids. What new information have you discovered about yourself recently? How did it reveal itself to you?

Chapter 15: The Things We Do...And Don't Do

Balancing what we give and what we expect is a delicate action. When have your found yourself questioning whether you have given too much help to your adult children? Do you question whether you give too much and are thwarting your AK's strive for confidence?

Chapter 16: Boundaries

In your parent-AK relationship, what issues or conversation topics are in need of "zip it" moments? How do you remind yourself at these times? Any special strategies you can share?

Chapter 17: Serious Troubles

What are your biggest take aways from the book? What behaviours will you change? What thinking has changed for you? What excites you most about the future with your adult children?

Chapter 18: We've Got This

Congratulate your friendship group on their contributions to your life with adult children. What special 'shares' have caused you to wonder, ponder or change?

Manufactured by Amazon.ca
Bolton, ON

41510165R00097